T0356464

Unraveling Your Relationship with MONEY

Unraveling Your Relationship with MONEY

Ditch Your Money Trauma So You Can Live an Abundant Life

SHANNAH GAME

WILEY

Library of Congress Cataloging-in-Publication Data

Names: Game, Shannah author
Title: Unraveling your relationship with money : discover (and ditch) your money trauma so you can live an abundant life / by Shannah Game.
Description: Hoboken, New Jersey : Wiley, [2025] | Includes index.
Identifiers: LCCN 2024036891 (print) | LCCN 2024036892 (ebook) | ISBN 9781394299850 Hardback | ISBN 9781394299874 epub | ISBN 9781394299867 adobe pdf
Subjects: LCSH: Finance, Personal | Money
Classification: LCC HG179 .G27 2025 (print) | LCC HG179 (ebook) | DDC 332.024—dc23/eng/20241031
LC record available at https://lccn.loc.gov/2024036891
LC ebook record available at https://lccn.loc.gov/2024036892

Cover Design: Paul McCarthy
SKY10094309_122324

To my tribe.
You know who you are.
Thank you!

Contents

Introduction

"Above all, be the heroine of your life, not the victim."

—Nora Ephron

There used to be an old-school wooden rollercoaster at Six Flags Magic Mountain named Colossus that makes me queasy just thinking about it. I've only ridden this beast a few times, but I've been terrified each time I set foot on the plank, ready to hop into the car. A few times, I've just turned around and chickened out (true story).

If you've ever been on an old wooden rollercoaster, you know how uncomfortable the ride is. Every twist and turn and bump you feel to the core of your body. The most horrifying part of the ride for me is the two- to three-second pause that happens just as you creep up the first hill before the first steep drop. I understand this is what rollercoaster enthusiasts live for, but why, I'll never quite understand. Each time I reach this stationary hang and the adrenaline starts to race through my body, I question how in the world I convinced myself this was a good idea.

The fear, panic, stress, and slight excitement at the top of the first hill on Colossus is kind of like what I call your relationship with money.

If the concept of having any kind of "relationship" with money is new to you, you've come to the right place. I've spent more than 20 years teaching, coaching, writing, and speaking about all things finance. I've learned one really important fact – money is always slightly terrorizing, even in the best of times, and utterly terrorizing in the worst of times. These strong feelings are what dictate your relationship with money: how you think, act, and feel about your finances. Your relationship with money is the foundation for every money decision you make and don't make.

Most people go their entire lives before they understand the power of their relationship with money. I get it. We're doing a pretty terrible job teaching financial literacy at a base level. Only 25 states currently require a standalone financial literacy class for high school students in the United States, so it may not be a surprise that many other countries, including Denmark, Sweden, Norway, and Canada, far surpass the United States in financial literacy education. Even with the best efforts, however, one thing that isn't taught in schools or universities or during your upbringing is how to deal with the mounting and heavy emotions around money. Why is this? That's a really good question, my friend, and one I've been searching for years to find the answers to.

Throughout my career, I've been deeply interested in how to help people just like you create change with their finances and, ultimately, lives. I often tell my students and coaching clients, if there isn't anything you want to do with your money or goals you want to reach, then learning about money should be put on the back burner. What does it matter in this situation? However, that's not reality. You've got stuff you want to do and aren't progressing toward it. And that just plain sucks. I think it's time to try a new approach because reading all the money how-to books, listening to all the podcasts, and scouring the internet for answers doesn't seem to be helping you create a well-lived life. If it were enough, you wouldn't still be searching for answers.

I'll let you in on a little secret. While I haven't done a formal poll of every human on earth, I'm guessing that most of us share a few common beliefs around money: (i) You can't enjoy life or feel happy unless you have a certain amount of money in your bank account. (ii) You feel you should be further along in your quest to build wealth. (iii) You feel like it's too late to learn about money, save for retirement, change careers, earn more money, pay off your debt, start a business, etc. (iv) You feel like there's never enough money to go around.

How would it feel to know that every person to your left and right shares these same core beliefs, no matter how much money they make or have?

Before you go shaming yourself for believing one of these common beliefs about money, I want to stop you. I'm writing this book to teach you about the power of your relationship with money and to help you discover that shame and judgment aren't emotions you need to hang onto anymore. I know that's easier said than done, and these days, everyone's a critic. But we're all out here trying to do our best, you included. So, if someone has not given you a permission slip to drop shame and judgment around money, let me be the first to offer this to you.

It's also hard to do because money is either the giant gray elephant in the room or the boogie monster, whichever feels most real to you. It's a taboo topic that you avoid talking about at all costs. You don't learn about money how-tos from your parents, mainly because they didn't learn about it from their parents, so the cycle of not talking about money continues for generations. This leads to trauma, fear, shame, regret, blame, judgment, panic, and so many other feelings that linger inside you. (Don't worry; we'll gently dive into all those feelings in this book.)

At this point, I'm sure you're asking yourself how you managed to be today years old before learning this. It's not your fault. Most money books leave out conversations about behavioral finance – the thoughts and feelings about money that are crucial building blocks in your financial plan. Instead, they teach how to save for your emergency fund. How to start investing in the stock market. How to buy a house. How to set up your 401(k). How to create a budget. And all of that stuff is great and helpful information to know, but if your relationship with money is messy, you don't have a chance at achieving your money goals. I know this to be true because that has been my story – even as a money expert – for years now. Before you can start to make better outward money decisions, you have to go inward and deal with your emotions.

If you feel like you've been treading water (or waking up in cold sweats) trying to pay off that credit card debt or wondering how you can save 20% for a down payment on that house you've been eyeing, let me give you some sweet relief: You are not broken. You have not made any original mistakes. You are not a failure when it comes to money. You are human and deeply intertwined with your relationship with money, formed when you came out of the womb. Your relationship with money is what's messed up – not you.

In this book, I'm going to talk about the other side of money. Beyond the numbers and spreadsheets and fancy mobile apps. I'm deeply interested in helping you do three things: (i) Heal your relationship with money so you let go of doing what you think is "right" with your money and start doing what you want to, (ii) Learn how to create a money plan that feels good and empowered, and (iii) Start building wealth toward the vision of life you have. How does that sound?

I also add a caveat that this book is not meant to serve as a quick fix or to suggest that changing your relationship with money will solve all your money problems. There are some real issues at play for many people, including poverty, homelessness, a lack of financial education, wage gaps, financial abuse, and more. Simply thinking better money thoughts won't solve those issues. However, whatever money situation you find yourself in, I want you to understand that this book is meant to introduce a different way of interacting with money. One that might be a little less stressful. A little less shameful. A little less judgmental. But a lot more empowering.

I've long searched for answers to help myself deal with money worries. I'm a money expert, and money is still a tricky subject for me, as you'll read in this book. Here's the Cliff Notes version of my life to show you that my road has been full of twists and turns: I started my first business in college, which collapsed during the dotcom bubble burst, was lost searching for a career, found my way to business school, got an MBA, started working with my dad in the financial industry, let my expenses get too high, took on $60K of graduate school debt, bought a house I couldn't really afford, got divorced, lost almost all of my assets and had to start over, spent way too much money (again), got remarried and moved into an expensive apartment, struggled financially in my business, started teaching financial literacy to thousands of students, started my podcast (which currently has more than 26 million downloads), had a miscarriage of twins that mentally devastated me for years, had an accident and became deaf in my left ear permanently and had to learn how to live with an invisible disability, moved across the country, and decided to write this book.

Ahhh, deep breath out! I share my story rather openly in this book to help you relate to the struggles that we all share around money. I've never met anyone whose money story was a solid upward line filled with only good things. That's both the beauty and the pain of living life; thankfully, we don't have to do it alone. We can work together.

The people's stories I share in this book are also meant to be an example of the hilarity and complexity around money. I've changed everyone's names and slight story details to keep my commitment to confidentiality. I hope you can see yourself in these stories and not feel alone.

So, if you're ready to shake loose all the suffering around money and embrace a new perspective, let's begin. This book is meant to be your guide and accompany you along the way because your relationship with money is a journey, not a destination. And while this book is about helping you unravel your relationship with money, I want to set some reasonable expectations. The pages in this book aren't a magical elixir to fix all things money. Despite my best efforts, I don't have a crystal ball for the future.

If you're feeling stuck financially, I encourage you to try all the exercises in this book and answer all the questions at the end of each chapter. Each chapter includes a Money Truth or Dare question, an Unraveling Thought, a Try This exercise, and Questions to Ponder. Little by little, I want you to move from feeling stressed or anxious about money to seeing light at the end of the tunnel. This book is personal to me but written for you. Once you start to feel a bit lighter about money, do me a favor and pass this book along to someone else. I'd love to start a movement of people who are ready to opt out of the status quo of negative self-talk and thinking around money and embrace a new way forward. Thanks for being a part of this movement!

Unraveling Your Relationship with MONEY

Why Is Your Relationship with Money Messed Up?

CHAPTER 1

How Do You Feel About Money?

nraveling your relationship with money. I hope I got your attention with the name of this book, and I hope it hits harder than other money books you might pick off the shelves. I promise you won't be overwhelmed by acronyms or money concepts that twist your brain in knots. This book is meant to open you up to exploring your thoughts and feelings around money in a way you may have never explored. I call it the other side of money. The journey with money we all take but never dare to talk about. What you'll read on these pages is an open diary of sorts as I work through my unhealthy relationship with money mixed with stories of real-life people on their journeys. Just like you, my relationship with money needed some serious unraveling, so I figured, let's do it together.

I hid like a scared child from my money for so many years that I couldn't keep count. Always waiting for the money boogie man to come out and grab me at every moment. Today, though, I knew it was different. It was time for me to start unraveling my relationship with money and face one of my biggest money fears.

I pulled into my bank in a sad, tired strip mall and was third in line for the drive-up ATM. I'm sure I was only in line for a few fleeting minutes, but it felt like a literal eternity. As I waited, I opened the sunroof on my shiny, black, over-priced BMW X5 and felt the fresh, warm evening air on my skin. I needed to feel alive at that moment. I peered into the backseat where my overstuffed blue suitcase, which was partially zipped closed, lay on the seat. I had gotten the car, which I nicknamed the "dream machine," just a few months prior in a moment of complete weakness. My dream car came with a very hefty monthly payment, making me blush to this day, but I didn't care; I had longed for that car for years. It somehow filled me up. That car took away, even briefly, the utter sense of loneliness and contempt for life that I felt. It made me feel grand and worthy, which a car should definitely not make you feel. (If you're going to compile a list of what *not* to do with your money, put this at the top: Never buy a car – or anything else – thinking it will fill the deep, dark black holes that exist in you. I promise you, it won't.) Have you ever made one of those purchase decisions that you knew was incredibly irrational, but you just didn't care? I'm sad to report that I've made a few of these decisions over the years that are cringeworthy at the very least.

We all do this, though. We make emotional and irrational choices with money to make ourselves feel better. This narrative of money's role in your life is ingrained in society. Turn on your TV, and you'll watch a series of commercials that try to sell you "the dream." You need a new car and a fancy one. You need a nice house, and a big one for sure. You need the latest gadget and the best shampoo; oh, and don't forget about the perfect credit card to buy all these things. Open up your favorite social media app, and within a second, your brain will trick you into believing you need to buy something to feel complete. Hold this thought; we'll get back here in a bit.

I could feel my heart racing, my palms sweaty as I gripped the black leather steering wheel and drove up to the ATM. I knew this had to be the moment that I finally decided to look at my ATM receipt . . . I just had to work up the courage. Every bone in my body screamed, "No, don't do it!" But this day, of all days, had to be the day I looked. You're probably thinking, "Wait, she's a money expert. Why is she not looking at her ATM receipts?" I have one of those brains that is a bit obsessive regarding numbers. It is my superpower when I'm helping other people figure out how to reach their money goals, but personally, it's sheer torture for me internally when it comes to looking at my numbers. But I'm not alone. The numbers make it real. The numbers tell the story of your money, good, bad, and everything in between. I used to spend so much time logging into my bank account with one eye open and a hand placed directly over where I knew the bank balance would be. The brain and body connection with money is real, palpable, and something we all feel to some extent.

The tattered, partially closed blue rectangular suitcase was a reminder of what being brave looked like. I had spent the previous tension-filled hours walking through my beloved brick house on the corner with the cutest front porch, perfectly landscaped backyard with a jacuzzi, and dreamlike hardwood floors, packing whatever belongings I could squeeze into that blue suitcase. I ripped through my closet, stuffing whatever I could grab in every crack and crevice. Tears ran down my face as I remembered a life I had wanted so badly but was now leaving behind. Pictures of a supposed happy couple on the red brick fireplace mantle now felt like someone else's life. This wasn't how my story was supposed to go. When I looked around one last time, I couldn't help but feel pity for all the stuff I bought over the years that was supposed to make me feel good. There was a collection of signature hardcover cookbooks from all around the world and beautiful artwork from Hawaii. My beloved cat, Sophie, was the hardest thing to leave. Sophie had been my companion for more than 10 years and always ensured I was okay. But, there was an odd sense of freedom in leaving it all behind. All this time, I was striving for a version of me buried under all that stuff. A version that was trapped inside the illusion of what I thought a wealthy life looked like. But then, I realized that money couldn't buy what I was searching for.

"Shannah, let's just get out of here as quick as possible," my dad said gently, his eyes full of tears and disgust. "Hold on, let me just stand here for a minute and think," I said as I looked around my soon-to-be former house. "Don't think too long, or you'll feel even worse," my mom said as she put the last of my shoes into the blue suitcase. "It's just stuff, I know, but it was my stuff, and now I don't have stuff, and I don't know how to feel about that," I spoke as my voice shook. What was this all for? And what is this strange feeling of release that rushed over my body? Sometimes, life can feel so unreal. Certain times in life feel like earth-shattering moments, which, in hindsight, are simply transitioning us into something new. Scary, yes. We can all do scary, though. That marked the end of my first marriage. Divorce was the next scary item on the agenda that I wasn't looking forward to.

Let me take you back, though. I worked as a Certified Financial Planner for years, helping people solve their money issues – paying off debt, improving credit scores, setting up retirement accounts, and creating budgets. I quickly learned that I should've gotten a degree in psychology instead of financial planning because money is *emotional*. Money is *irrational*. Money keeps you stuck in an endless loop of negative self-talk and thinking. We all tell stories in our head about money and, trust me, those stories are not uplifting and helpful. They are often untrue and destructive. Why do we do this, you might ask. Well, money holds power over you. Money keeps you out of rooms that you deserve to be in. Money divides lines and evokes anger, stress, and trauma. Money is always there. It is inescapable. Money touches every aspect of life, whether you like it or not.

. . .

TRY THIS...

I love wearing necklaces. But every time I go to put one on, I spend about 20 minutes cussing up a storm, straining my eyes to try to get it untangled. It's maddening because I act like I never know how or why that knot is there, but deep down, I know that it would be so easy to keep it untangled if I stored it differently. How you feel about money is just like that knotted necklace. There may even be so many tangles in your relationship with money that you aren't even sure which one came first. This exercise will help you start to untangle.

Get out a blank piece of paper. At the top, title it "How I Feel About Money." For 15-ish minutes, write down every thought that comes to mind about your feelings toward money. It's important not to judge yourself during this process, so swing for the fences and let all your feelings out. When the time is up, take a minute and read back what you wrote again without judging yourself. Next, step away from that piece of paper for at least 24 hours to give your brain a break from these intense feelings. But in the meantime, give yourself a little pep talk. Say affirmations like "You are taking brave and bold steps to heal your relationship with money. You've got this." When it's time to go back to that paper, see if you can find a common thread that connects your feelings. You might find a consistent theme of happiness, curiosity, or intrigue, or on the negative side, fear, shame, guilt, or anxiety. Whatever you find, keep in mind that your feelings are yours, they're legitimate, and you do not need to justify them to anyone.

Once you see the bigger picture about your money feelings, ask yourself, "Why do I feel this way?" Here's an example: Let's say your common thread is one of the most common feelings: shame. You want to dig a bit deeper and see if you can get to the bottom of why that shame exists. Is it because you have student loan debt, made a not-so-good investment, or had to close down a business? Maybe the shame comes from not feeling you're where you should be in life. Keep digging deeper and deeper by repeating the question, "Why do I feel this way?" until you feel like you have a general sense of where these feelings originate from. Now you have something to work with.

THE STORY OF MONEY

The crazy part about money is that it is man-made. Coins and paper money were invented in China around 770 BCE and when currency replaced bartering for the trade of goods and services, it opened the door to a system that changed the world so significantly that now, almost 3000 years later, those simple pieces of paper still hold tremendous influence in our lives. We almost never touch money anymore. Coins and paper money have been replaced with a touch of a button, removing any decision-making in the process. Money almost doesn't feel real these days. We're living in a world where access to money has become easier and easier but the emotions around money have only become more and more complicated.

Though essential as money is, it's not something we talk about much. When you describe a friend, you don't say, "Barbara is tall, has brown hair and green eyes, is super-lovable, and enjoys eating ramen and playing air hockey. And she has money." It's just not a descriptor that we would use to describe someone in a typical situation. What this tells me is that money is something we need, but it's not who we are.

But even if money is technically just used for business transactions, many of us attach some heavy feelings to those bills – and they aren't happy rainbows and sunshine daydreams. The most important thing I want you to understand is that if you have negative feelings of dread, shame, or failure around money, it's not your fault. (Read that again.) Because you're a human raised in a money-driven culture, you've been programmed to think and feel a certain way about money from the moment you take your first breath to the moment you take your last. (And sometimes even after, if you've ever been involved in distributing an estate.) If you spend those breaths in between with nothing but negative thoughts about money, you'll be stuck in patterns that aren't good for your mind, body, or soul.

So how do you begin to look at money subjectively when it feels so impossible to separate yourself from it?

. . .

MONEY TRUTH OR DARE: (PICK ONE OR DO BOTH)

TRUTH: What's one money secret you have that you've never shared with anyone?
DARE: Ask a friend or family member this same question and share your truth.

. . .

MONEY AND YOUR EMOTIONS

Throughout the years, I noticed a very strange phenomenon. Clients who had what you would refer to as a "sh*t-ton" of money were often incredibly insecure and unhappy. They were always worried about running out of money or being unable to keep up their shiny exterior status and even suffered from panic attacks and nightmares. On the other hand, clients who were just getting by, just making ends meet, were often incredibly secure and happy. It didn't make sense to me then, but now I understand it so well. Money is a feeling, not a number. It's easy to believe that money is binary. You simply input what you want and line up the amount of money it will cost to get what you want. If money were binary, we'd all have it figured out long before now. Achieving your goals would be a simple math equation. But you and I both know it's just not that simple.

That ping in your chest when you open your bank account or that utter sense of defeat when you don't have enough money to do something you really want to do is normal and rational. Money is a primal need, like food, air, and water. As much as you'd like to say money doesn't matter, it does. But the issue is that you operate largely with a scarcity mindset because our entire financial system was set up to have you believe you will never have enough money, never achieve your goals, it's always too late, and you will always be behind.

It never mattered how much money someone had, their age, their demographic, the car they drove, or the house they lived in. I learned we all suffer from the same money fears, worries, anxieties, and negative thoughts about money, just like Jim and Sarah.

I'd like to introduce you to Jim and Sarah.

The couple initially hired me to help them build their credit score, but as I began my meeting with them, I knew there was more to the story. As we sat across from each other at their 10-ft-long solid wood dining table with perfectly arranged centerpieces of perfectly plucked red roses, their energy was undeniable. Something was bubbling up under the surface, and it was coming in hot – they didn't need a financial planner, they needed a money therapist.

"So tell me, what's going on?" I asked, hoping to cut the tension in the air. "I don't know, this is the first I've heard of any money issues, so Jim, why don't you explain what's really going on here," Sarah exclaimed with her arms crossed and a look on her face that meant business.

"Okay," he said. He took a breath, and it all came pouring out like a dam that had burst under too much pressure. "We have about ten credit cards, and I've maxed them out. I always sign up for a new credit card whenever I get a new offer and use it until it is maxed out, then repeat the process. Money is pretty tight right now, but I just need to figure out how to raise our credit score so I can get another credit card to shuffle around some of this debt," Jim said as beads of sweat visibly showed on his forehead. "I run a business, and I make really good money. I just need this fix to help us get out of this money crunch, and then I'll figure out how to pay everything off."

"Wait, you have been doing what?!" Sarah asked, her eyes wide. "Where does all the money that you make each month go? Isn't that a lot of money? How could we not be able to pay our bills? Jim, this doesn't make any sense to me. Why is this the first time I'm learning about it?"

I could tell this money secret had been silently torturing Jim for months if not years. The shame he felt coming clean made me want to run up to him and give him the biggest bear-hug possible. Of course, I just sat still and continued to listen.

"No, that isn't possible, Jim. You have a good job, you run a business, and we have lots of money; what in the world are you talking about?" Sarah said now in a full-on scream rage. Jim turned my way sheepishly, almost begging me with his dark brown eyes to somehow take away the pain of this moment. "I'm sorry," was all he had left to say.

"Look, we're not going to get anywhere by blaming each other now. Let's focus on what we can do. How about you start by telling me honestly the emotions, fears, and thoughts about money you're having right now," I said gently. Over the next hour, Jim and Sarah let down their guard and invited me into their private world of money thoughts, beliefs, and the reality of where their money was going. Jim wanted

Sarah and his kids to have the best life possible because he didn't have many financial resources growing up, but he went to extremes to make that happen, including the 10 credit cards with massive debt. Oppositely, Sarah grew up wealthy and believed that money would never run out because she was owed a good life. Her kids would attend prestigious universities, and she would always live in a nice house, drive the fanciest of cars, and have jewels to die for. She didn't want to keep up with the Joneses, she wanted to *be* the Joneses. They had been married for 15 years, and this was the first time they had an honest, nonjudgmental conversation about their real feelings about money. The credit cards were what I call the tip of the iceberg. They were the red light flashing issue that bubbled up to the surface, but I'm always more interested in what's going on under the surface because that's where your money feelings live. To make outward changes around money, you – for better or worse – need to spend some time down there.

. . .

UNRAVELING THOUGHT #1

You cannot change your money situation when you are stuck in shame and judgment of yourself and other people.

. . .

You're probably wondering, did she ever look at the ATM receipt? I'll give you the answer. But first, a story.

I spent a ridiculous amount of time on YouTube looking up how to create easy origami shapes in seconds, and the crane was my go-to. Each time I'd pull a receipt out of the machine I would immediately transform it into a crane before my eyes could glance at the numbers. I shoved all those little cranes into the dark crevices of my wallet, where they stayed tucked away until they found themselves in the trash can. I never looked at one ATM receipt in more than 10 years. Yep, 10 YEARS!

This is why money doesn't make sense. I always had enough money in my bank account to pay my bills, so I didn't look because

I didn't have to. Despite that reassurance, though, my brain still walked through every disastrous situation that could happen. I started endlessly subtracting the bills that I had to pay: $2,000 for my mortgage, $250 for electricity, $100 for cable, $300 a week for groceries, and $950 for that BMW payment (I know). Even if it wasn't the reality, I pictured myself with $0 left and suddenly, I was destitute in my head because I couldn't pay my bills. I would have to give up my house, file for bankruptcy, and explain to everyone why this so-called money expert found herself penniless and homeless. I don't know where that life-altering scenario, a complete money lie, originated, but it was real. Despite never experiencing that situation in my entire life, the fear of being broke kept me locked in a fight-or-flight response around money. My heart would race, my cheeks would get flushed and turn into a deep shade of cherry red, and my hands would get shaky. This reaction was happening internally to a fake external occurrence that I knew in my gut would never happen, but my brain and body believed otherwise. I can't rationalize it – I don't even know where it came from. But the origin for your fake failure scenario doesn't matter when you're in the throes of a near panic attack.

On that life-changing day, I slowly rolled down my window and punched in my ATM passcode as slowly as I possibly could. My heart was about to leap out of my chest. I snatched the receipt, forgoing any origami animals this time, and drove recklessly to the first parking spot I could find. Just then, "Where the Streets Have No Name" by U2, only the best song ever written, came on the radio. I blasted the song and sang at the top of my lungs. *I want to run. I want to hide. I want to tear down these walls that hold me inside.* Was it a sign that this moment was the time to start unraveling my relationship with money?

There was no turning back. "Look at the numbers on 3, 2, 1. . . Okay, it wasn't that bad," I thought as I breathed deeply. In fact, it was pretty good. There was more money in my bank account than I had guessed. Had I dodged a bullet? The blood rushed back into my body and I realized that I'd been holding my breath for the entire time. I was going to live another day.

Did I cure myself of the fear of looking at my ATM receipts that day? Cue the confetti. Not even close. But it was a start. And sometimes a start is the best, and only, step you can take.

. . .

 YOUR RELATIONSHIP WITH MONEY IS. . .

A conversation with Matt Schulz, author of *Ask Questions, Save Money, Make More*, and chief credit analyst at LendingTree.

Shannah: If you had to describe your relationship to money as a cartoon character, who would it be?

Matt: I think that the first thing that really came to mind was maybe like Lisa Simpson. Someone who always tries to do the right thing, but doesn't always quite get it right and has had their stumbles in the past. I feel like that might be a good choice because I'm somebody who had $10,000 in credit card debt when I was in my 20s and basically wrecked my life for several years. I also had a car payment on a brand-new car at that time because of a bad decision, and I just hope that you can learn through those mistakes and the mistakes of others and come out the other side.

Shannah: Tell me, how do you feel about money?

Matt: I've had a complicated relationship with money, and my general feeling is that it really is about the freedom of having more money and being able to put some money aside and save. It's a school of thought that, if you make enough money to not worry about paying all the bills at the end of the month, that's a hugely freeing thing. If you have a horrible job and you're being treated poorly by your boss, you can tell him to shove it and leave with confidence because you have savings, that is freedom. And there are so many other examples like that, so I guess I would kind of look at it that way. I try to also pay that forward, whether it's donating financially or paying the knowledge forward, and that's certainly a theme of the book, too.

Shannah: If you could get a do-over for one money mistake, what would it be?

Matt: Honestly, I probably would have been smarter about how I handled things in my 20s and not run up the debt that I had. I certainly would not have bought that car. Living in a town like Austin that has exploded over the past 20–25 years, I might have bought a couple of pieces of property back then – and even taken on debt to do it – because I would have come out just fine. But yeah, I think I would probably go back to that credit card spending in my 20s. That really put me behind the eight-ball for a while.

. . .

What you think about money matters. Those thoughts turn into feelings that drive your actions, patterns, and behaviors with money. Want to know why you set a money goal to save, invest, or pay off debt only to find yourself saying, "Well, I'm never going to reach that goal, so let's just go out and spend money; I'll feel much better"? That dopamine hit you get from spending money is exciting and addictive. It makes you feel good, and you are wired to want nice things and to feel good. The work comes in finding the space between "Forget it, I want to spend money" and "I should really save," and navigating the complex emotions behind money. There is a softness and intentionality you can welcome that hits you right in the dopamine receptors, too. But it is going to take some work. Don't worry; I'll hold your hand along the way.

QUESTIONS TO PONDER

1. How do you feel about money?
2. How do you want to feel about money?
3. What's holding you back from feeling good about money?
4. How would your life change if you swapped negative feelings for positive ones?

CHAPTER **2**

Would You Date
Your Money?

"Money isn't everything." It is a great bumper sticker tagline, but honestly, it is pretty hard to put into practice every day if you're worrying about paying your bills.

The reality is that money touches every aspect of our lives. At the least we need it to keep the lights on and the water running, but its impact is far greater. Beyond everyday living, money is the access point to doing those *other* things in life, like traveling, seeing a movie, attending a concert, or going out to eat with friends. Money decides what you get to do and what you don't. Money dictates where you live and whom you live with. Money is inescapable despite your best efforts.

Money comes with a wide range of emotions, from fear, shame, and guilt to joy, excitement, and hope. You can feel all these emotions and more about money on a given day – and sometimes all at once.

A friend of mine reached out to me, freaking out about money. I asked her what was going on during the day. She shared that she had been laid off from her job, got a parking ticket in a spot she always parks in when she runs to grab her favorite coffee, and then came home and realized she had forgotten to pay the electric bill she didn't set up for autopay. Right after that news, she got an email that she had won a $500 Amazon gift card from a survey she filled out a few months prior. While the gift card didn't take away her money worries, she was so confused at how she could feel both fear, anger, and excitement about money all within a couple of hours. Given her circumstances, I assured her that these are all very normal emotions to feel and offered her permission to sit and just feel those feelings. She didn't need to try to fix anything right at that moment. Her only task was to be human and allow her body to experience whatever it needed to experience.

You've probably never thought about your relationship with money until you picked up this book. You might not have realized that you even have a relationship with money. Spoiler alert: You do, and if you're going to have a relationship, why not make it a damn good one?

It's funny how easy it is to settle for a pretty crappy relationship with money. When someone asks me why your relationship with money matters, I offer this as a selling point. Let's say you can create the love of your life. Give me some characteristics you would like this person to embody – charming, good-looking, fun to be around, successful, easy to talk to, etc. What is probably *not* on that list are qualities like this – constantly puts me down, tells me all the horrible things about myself, encourages me to create unhealthy patterns, and keeps me locked in a chronic state of fear, shame, regret, etc. So, if you wouldn't accept these qualities in your love life, why in the world would you accept them in your relationship with money?

Doug and Heather Boneparth, a husband-wife team at Bone Fide Wealth and authors of *The Joint Account* newsletter, believe that we excuse bad relationships with money because we can. "Money doesn't cry. Money doesn't judge. You don't worry about disappointing your accounts the way you would someone you love. Plus, society gives you lots of ways to avoid your deeper issues with money if you have them: credit cards, buy-now-pay-later programs, even autopay for your bills, which while convenient, removes the consciousness from examining your spending behaviors. There are bandages you can apply to pretend you're not hurting. In a sense, fixing your finances might be just as hard as fixing a damaged relationship – you can't always control the timeline around things getting better," they shared. It takes time to cultivate new practices around money in a relationship and access to a judgment-free zone where you agree to collectively drop the shame and blame. I know, I get it. Having "the money talk" with your partner never quite makes it to the top of the to-do list. You don't have to jump in all at once. Slow and steady does win the race.

· · ·

 MONEY TRUTH OR DARE

TRUTH: Is the way you are spending money causing you or others stress? How so?
DARE: Take $20 (or whatever amount feels good to you) from your bank account and move it to your savings or investments today.

· · ·

GET TO KNOW YOUR MONEY

I'm pretty confident that you and your money have operated as separate entities until now. Maybe you're in a really good place with money and don't feel it needs much attention. Maybe you're in a tough spot with money and don't want to give it any attention. Both are fair scenarios, and I would say most people fall into one of those categories. Either way, we can all agree that we'd much rather have our money just work in the background, doing what it's supposed to do and being there when we need it to be, than have to manage it.

Getting to know your money is an important part of unraveling your relationship with money and ultimately helping you reach your money goals (or live the life you want). What does it mean to get to know your money? I'm not talking about logging in to look at your bank account balance. That's good to do, don't get me wrong. Getting to know your money is understanding it from all dimensions.

Emotionally: What are your central thoughts and feelings around money, where do they come from, where do you feel money stress in your body, how does money impact your relationships, career, health, sleep, and more, how do you soothe yourself in moments of money stress, do you overspend or underspend as an emotional response, what's your biggest money fear, what gets you excited about money, etc. There are SO many things to consider from an emotional standpoint when you're getting to know your money. I guess you've never thought about many items on the list above. That's okay. This is the inner work around money that is so often overlooked.

Financially: What is your net worth, how much are you saving in your retirement plan, what is your biggest monthly expense, what's your debt payoff strategy, what's your plan to afford college for your kids, do you have your financial risks covered, how much do you need for retirement, and how much do you have in your emergency fund are just a few of the financial items on your get-to-know-your-money checklist. This is the outer work around money.

Imagine going on a date with someone and not discovering anything about them. How weird of an experience would that be? I want you to consider if you're giving your money that same silent treatment.

I do not want you to nerd out on everything money, or get so obsessed that you drive yourself crazy. I think a healthy level of curiosity is the sweet spot I'm going for.

THE FIRST DATE

If you've ever tried online dating, you know what a complete cluster fuck it can be. There are so many no's to try to get to a yes. I had spent a solid year in therapy after my divorce, and trust me, going to therapy every week was a big financial (and emotional) commitment. I wanted to learn more about myself and do what I could to cultivate a healthy relationship with my next partner. In one of my first therapy appointments post-divorce, in between endless tissues to sop up my tears of sadness, my therapist offered a unique suggestion. She wanted me to write what she called The List. The List could be as long or as short as I'd like, detailing all the qualities I hoped to find in someone I wanted to spend my life with. This list wasn't to be a fairytale version of relationships like I saw on TV, but a solid list of what I wanted most in a partner – the real stuff.

I picked up a meatball sandwich from my favorite Italian restaurant with a double order of French fries, grabbed a glass of wine, and sat down that evening to write The List. Over the next few hours, I wrote down anything I thought of without second-guessing myself. Interestingly, I found it pretty easy to list everything I *didn't* want in a partner – lazy, easily angered, not into sports, couldn't cook, wasn't nice or encouraging, etc. Coming up with what I *did* want was a harder task. By now, I distinctly understood that looks come and go and money can be fleeting. After working for five years in the financial industry up until that point, I had worked with a lot of people who hoped they'd marry someone who would financially support them, only to have relationships end in divorce, death, disability, and more. Instead of money, I wanted to find someone who would be with me no matter what happened in life but who was also equally motivated to create a good life. Thinking about the kind of partner I wanted to share my life with, beyond career and money, was something I hadn't thought about previously. I think I always bought into the fairytale of a princess meeting her prince and riding off into the sunset happily ever after without a care in the world. Cue the *whomp-whomp* sound effects. I know this illusion isn't reality.

As I wrote out The List, I couldn't help but think of the similarities with my relationship with money. What role did I want money to play in my life? Would I "date my money" if it always talked down to me, like it had for years before? What relationship with money was I engaged in, and did I have a choice? I wasn't ready to tackle my relationship with money at that point in my life. It was scary enough to think about finding a love match. Honestly, I should've been more focused on my relationship with money. I wish I had understood on an intimate level the concepts and ideas I'm sharing with you in this book. It might've saved me a lot of money in credit card debt and countless hours of deep, dark worry, shame, fear, and regret.

. . .

 UNRAVELING THOUGHT #2

You are in a life-long, deeply enmeshed relationship with money.
You get to decide what that looks like. Why not make it a good one?

. . .

LOVE, PART 2

I first saw Jeff's face, my current husband, when I set up my online profile on Match.com. I had just finished writing The List a few days prior. It was New Year's Eve, and I had nowhere to go but my couch, with a tub of cookie dough in hand and a bottle of champagne to drink. I turned *Dick Clark's New Year's Rockin' Eve* up full blast and headed to my computer in my office to write my Match.com profile. I uploaded a few recent pictures that looked like me with a cute little profile and hit the post button. I walked back to the kitchen for a champagne refill, and within a few seconds, the computer beeped, letting me know I had my first few matches. Nervously, I read through all the matches between bites of cookie dough. I had seen Jeff's profile that night, but there were two problems. One, he lived about 50 miles away, which, if you know anything about how terrible it is to get anywhere on

Los Angeles freeways, did not sound like a good idea. Let alone the gas money I'd spend to see him would be a big budget addition. Second, I was only going to reply to matches that first sent me a message. So I did what was the only logical thing to do: ignore his perfectly good profile and gravitate toward some of the other responses I had gotten that I *knew* were not going to be good matches.

You know how this story goes. I went on a few pretty bad dates with perfectly good men, just not men who were good for me. One of the best of the worst was with a guy who appeared like a "perfect" match on paper. He had a great job, made good money, and was interested in many things I was interested in – travel, good food, friends, etc. We met at a restaurant across the street from where I lived for an early evening drink at the bar. When the waitress came over to our table to take the order, he ordered a drink without pause. Now, I'm a perfectly capable, stand on my own two feet, kind of woman, but on a first date, I'd love it if I could order first. After he ordered, he said, "Oh, yes, I guess I'll buy you a drink. Go ahead and order something like a glass of wine." That was strike one in my book. Not that I expected him to buy me anything, but how he offered up the suggestion rubbed me the wrong way. I knew this was not my guy, so I turned the conversation into a question-and-answer session as if he were a client. "What do you do for a living?" "What do you do for fun?" "What's an experience that you've enjoyed in life?" Thirty minutes later, after one drink, we mutually accepted that this would not be a love match, shook hands, and parted ways. The very next day, I went on a date with Jeff, and as they say, the rest is history.

My first kiss with Jeff was a gushy love scene from a rom-com; I'm certain of it. I had driven down to his apartment on a Sunday afternoon in late January for our second date, deep into the NFL football playoffs. Walking to his apartment that afternoon, I wondered what I was doing going to his house for a second date. I drove 50 miles to some strange man's apartment and was about to spend the afternoon with him. I thought about turning around so many times. Isn't this how women get killed in all the horror movies? Even with extreme skepticism, I was determined to see what this day could bring. What's the worst that can happen, I thought. (Yes, I know, a lot. I wouldn't suggest this move after just meeting someone online.)

Wearing a white Beatles T-shirt, Jeff answered the door with a big smile, "You're here!" He lived just a few short blocks from the long sandy beach in Long Beach, California, and you could feel the cool, damp, salt-filled air throughout his apartment as he held open the door. "Hey, I was thinking, why don't we get cupcakes before eating dinner? I know a great place with the best red velvet cupcakes with cream cheese frosting," he said. We had a conversation on our first date about how much I loved dessert and that my motto in life was always to have dessert first, so let's just say I was already feeling the love vibes from this suggestion. As we made our way down to the cupcake shop, I started to think about a future life together. We could buy a cute little love shack near the beach, drink margaritas on our deck, and pop out a couple of kids in a few years. I hoped he had a great credit score and at least a retirement plan. I gave mine up in my divorce and was 34 years old without any retirement savings. Not an ideal financial situation to be in. A cushy retirement plan wasn't on The List, but still, I was hopeful.

Cupcakes turned into dinner at his apartment, complete with a conversation about life, money, and purpose. It's par for the course when you're dating a money expert that the topic of money will come up quickly. We grew up entirely differently, the yin to my yang. Jeff shared how his family always just got by. But they had everything they needed. He had these big dreams of becoming a journalist and writing about his favorite musicians, like the great *Rolling Stone* writers he'd idolized for years. I had a saying that I shared with a few of my closest friends as I started to date again after my divorce. I want to find a partner who, in the worst-case scenario, would care for me and make me laugh even if we had to live in a cardboard box on the side of the road. That quality was for sure on The List. This feeling marked a significant change from how I used to value all that stuff and money the years before. It felt like a new and fresh perspective, and I was committed to honoring it.

As the clock struck midnight, Jeff walked me to my ridiculously overpriced black dream machine of a car parked just a few blocks from his apartment. The beach air turned into a fine mist that danced through the sky that night. It was so quiet outside I swear you could hear a pin drop. I opened my front car door, flung my purse into the passenger seat, and turned around. Before I knew what was happening, Jeff grabbed my cheeks to come in for a kiss. Our first kiss. It was as close to perfection of a first kiss as I could imagine.

. . .

 ## YOUR RELATIONSHIP WITH MONEY IS. . .

A conversation with Doug Boneparth, Certified Financial Planner, founder of Bone Fide Wealth and co-author of *The Millennial Money Fix, and The Joint Account,* and Heather Boneparth, lawyer, co-author of *The Millennial Money Fix, The Joint Account* and writer of *Our Tiny Rebellions*

Shannah: Who would it be if you had to describe your relationship with money as a famous TV couple?

Doug: I don't know how famous they are, but if you remember the cartoon show Rugrats the Pickles and Tommy Pickle, the baby, that's how I would describe my relationship with money. The mother was the bread-earning wife with a corporate job. I think she was an attorney, and the father was an entrepreneur and a toy inventor. I'm not a toy inventor, but you know the vibe is the same.

Shannah: What's one money mistake that you wish you could get a do-over for?

Heather: That's an easy layup question for me. I took out $200,000 to attend a very expensive law school in New York City without fully understanding what it meant to be a lawyer or how I wanted to use that degree. It took me a very, very long time to reconcile my feelings around that and to get control of the debt.

Shannah: Tell me your inner monologue about money. Is there a money thought that always plays in a loop for you?

Heather: Somebody just asked me what my money motto is, and I said it's the Beyonce song where she goes, "Move out the way I'm with my girls, and we all need space," and I would say that that's my money motto. It's why I joined Doug, and why I'm doing what I'm doing. It's really about finding more significant equity, giving a more extraordinary voice, to not only define that voice for myself, but for other women, who may have lost it along the way, whether that's professionally or through becoming a mother and trying to redefine for our next act. I would say my inner monologue is mostly Beyonce.

Shannah: If you could go back and tell your younger self something about money, what would it be?

Doug: My brother and I were both very, very good at making money. As the entrepreneurial spirit ran deep generationally down to us, I would have told myself to invest that money. We made such good money as teenagers, and I had a lot of fun. I never needed to ask my parents for anything. I could fill the car with gas; I could go to the movies, do whatever I wanted to do. But I was not taught, ironically, even with a financial advisor, to take a portion of the money and invest it. If I had, I probably could have been in a much better situation at any part of my life.

. . .

 TRY THIS...

I want you to write The List for your relationship with money. Consider the qualities you want your money to possess for your money list. This may seem odd. Just hear me out. It's a great exercise to get you thinking differently, and objectively, about your relationship with money. Using my example of writing out The List for a romantic relationship, it's often easier to think about what you don't want. Here are some examples that might spur your thinking:

I don't want:

- Fear
- Shame
- Regret
- To run out of money
- To not take risks
- To be scared of the future
- To be envious of others
- To lack money
- Judgment
- To feel overwhelmed
- Confusion

Now that you've listed what you don't want, let's focus on what you do want. This should be more fun. I understand that money is not a person, but for this exercise, it might help to picture money as if it were a person, just like you were entering any other relationship. Here are some examples to spur your thinking:

I do want:

- Joyful
- Connected
- Always present
- Fulfilled
- Overflowing
- Excited for the future
- Encouraged
- Say nice things to me (yes, this is possible)
- Put to good use
- Working to fund my goals
- Intentional
- Focused
- Giving to others

How did you feel doing this exercise? Thinking about money from this perspective can be a stretch because this is all new territory. This exercise is meant to encourage you to think about your current relationship with money versus what you want. How big is the divide between those two realities? You'll have lots of time to work on the "how" piece of this divide, but I just want you to know what you want and what's missing.

YOUR MIND ON MONEY

You have a money mindset, or how you think, act, and feel about money. Your money mindset is shaped by how you were raised, your decisions, your general outlook on life, friends, family, experiences, and so much more. It's complex and difficult to unravel.

Being mindful of your money, life, career, relationships, etc., starts with setting aside time to regroup and direct your focus toward positive, empowering thoughts and taking progressive action to be the best version of yourself. By rewiring your thoughts, you form positive habits that can lead to success. It's not really about what you want but what you are willing to do to get what you want – and you must start somewhere.

Your money mindset holds incredible power over you. Whether you know it or not, it already does. Your money mindset can be your best friend and tell you positive and reaffirming statements such as, "Hey, you are awesome for making that extra payment toward your credit card last week," or "It's okay if you don't get that raise; you're doing a great job – keep at it." These affirming thoughts can go a long way toward keeping you centered, stress-free, and focused on seeing the good.

Your money mindset can also be your worst nightmare, replaying repeatedly in your mind, reminding you of all the money mistakes you've made and affirming that "you will never get out of debt" or "you have a real shopping problem, you know." These money lies keep you stuck in the cycles you so desperately want to break, like overspending, being afraid to spend, debt, undervaluing your worth, and more.

Cultivating a healthy money mindset starts with mindfulness. Mindfulness is a practice of actively paying attention to what you are focusing on and any judgments you are making as a result of that focus. You can do mindfulness throughout the day: while you're at your job, exercising, making money decisions about buying a house, or are out at dinner. You can practice money mindfulness in big moments when you're faced with what feels like a life-altering dilemma or in the small, in-between moments when making daily money decisions.

The critical thing to remember is to start small. Mindfulness is like exercising a muscle. Sure, you could start with the 20-pound weights first, but chances are you won't be able to do too many reps, if any at all. You'll most likely end up discouraged and frustrated, and you probably won't want to try again. Instead, start with 2-pound weights, then move on to 5-pound weights, 10-pound weights, and so on until you build muscle.

Building a healthy money mindset is the same as building muscle: You need to start small. You build that healthy mindset muscle each time you choose to be kind to yourself or put $20 extra toward your debt this month. These small money mindset choices will build over time to create a healthier, stronger mindset and the ability to take bigger steps.

There are many ways to shift from a negative mindset to a positive one. It starts with replacing negative thoughts with positive ones. For example, use the "This/Not That" list on the next page as examples of changing negative thought patterns into positive ones.

Create your own list of "This/Not That" items when negative thought patterns come up. But don't stop there.

This

- I'm going to put $20 toward my debt this week
- I am going to listen to a podcast this week about women in the workplace
- I am going to write a list of 10 things I love about where I live

Not That

- I will never get out of debt
- I don't know how to negotiate for a raise
- I will never be able to buy a home

Creating a healthy mindset is also about taking time out of your day to center yourself and focus your attention on something that is calming and nourishing to your soul.

Here are a few examples of ways to add more mindfulness to your day:

- Think kind, loving thoughts about where you are at in life
- Do a simple breathing exercise to spur relaxation and peace
- Go for a gratitude walk and list 10 things you're grateful for
- Head to a yoga class to clear your mind
- Listen to a playlist that inspires you
- Meditate for at least 10 minutes with your favorite app
- Stop what you are doing and reconnect with your goals
- Remind yourself of all the good decisions you have made this year
- Cook a great meal and savor each bite

When you are mindful of your money, you are actively deciding where to put your focus. Redirecting your focus puts you in the driver's seat to decide how you will spend your money, what goals are important in your life, and how you choose to frame your current money situation. It doesn't mean you will never have a setback or a slip-up. Instead, a good money mindset is the art of making peace with your money and the decisions you have made, knowing that when you do slip up, you dust yourself off, refocus your goals, and move forward without all the negative self-talk – the key ingredients to any good relationship with money.

Real change comes from being mindful every day and focusing on positive thoughts like, "It's okay, I'll make a better decision next time," or heading out for a walk when you are stressed out and anxious about money. You will be surprised at the change and progress you can make once you commit to getting into a good relationship with your money mindset.

MONEY AND THE MYTHS

There are so many similarities between dating relationships and money relationships. We tend to put up with relationships that aren't good for us. Relationships that don't nurture us. We accept less than we're worth. When it comes to money, we easily attach ourselves to money myths that we believe are true but ultimately hurt our chances of having a healthy and strong relationship. You might recognize some of these money myths in your relationship with money. I want to encourage you to examine how these common money myths show up in your relationship with money and hinder your progress toward your goals. Or keep you in a place of shame, fear, blame, guilt, etc.

Here are some of the common money myths that we let dictate our relationship with money.

Myth #1 – Money is only about math. You know by now that's not true. Eighty to ninety percent of your money habits and beliefs are based on your thoughts and feelings about money. (Read that again.) If being financially successful was only about math, we'd all have money figured out. It would be a simple plug-and-play application with money. Money is so much more complicated than the math piece, and I'm ready to destroy this myth so you can finally build a healthy relationship with money. Financial literacy (the understanding of how money works) plus emotional intimacy go hand-in-hand to create a solid equation for money success.

Myth #2 – Wealthy is a number. Again, so not true. I've helped so many people who had a ton of money, like hundreds of millions of dollars, and they don't feel wealthy. I know it sounds cliché, but wealth is really about every aspect of your life – your health, money, thoughts, hobbies, career, family and friends, etc. And . . . how you use your money to help you live the life you want. You can build wealth and be wealthy on any salary – I can prove that to you. The starting point is figuring out what wealth means to you.

Years ago, I had a money client who was 24 and working in her first job. She was a social worker and loved what she did, but she only made $32,000. She lived in New York City, and her rent comprised more than 70% of her take-home pay. She had a few thousand dollars of student loan debt that she took out and was paying off. She hired me for an hour to review her finances and let her know if she was optimizing her money. What I saw, I was envious of. She plans her meals weekly and uses mobile apps to save on groceries. She was contributing to her 401(k) up to her company match. She used her credit card like a debit card, paying off the monthly balance and racking up many points. She used those points to pay for her family and friends' gift cards when they had a birthday. She had an emergency fund and set up a fun fund, as I call it, for money she could blow however she wanted without guilt. She was using her company's perk that offered her up to $5,000 in continuing education every year. She was intentional with her money and a pro at working through her feelings about money. I didn't have a lot of notes for her. She was thriving, much more so than other clients earning $500,000+. She felt wealthy, and that's what mattered.

Is wealth a number, a feeling, or a little of both? And once you reach your definition of wealth . . . will you actually feel wealthy? These are all personal questions without a right or wrong answer.

Myth #3 – Achieving your goals is only about saving money. WRONG. Being smart and intentional with your money is far more about how you spend money. Most of us are bad at intentionally spending money because money is so emotional. Here's the classic pattern of events. You spend money when you feel good and when you don't, and everything in between, without much thought behind it. Here's a great little exercise to try. Pick one thing you spent money on and say, "This week I spent x dollars on x things. That's fascinating." No judgment or shame; just bring awareness to how you spend your money. Don't be surprised if you feel shocked when you uncover how much you are spending on certain things. However, you usually start passing blame on yourself, so you're never really motivated to see where and how you are spending money. Don't do that. Just become aware of how you choose to spend your money.

Myth #4 – Your parents are better at money than you are. I love this one personally. Listen, you're here learning about money, bettering yourself, and working through the emotions around money. Most of our parents never were taught any of this. They surely weren't taught about money in school. Your parents are also trying to figure it out with less information or access to information about financial literacy. It's perfectly okay to share your money goals and milestones with your parents but remember, their advice might not be the best advice for you. I'm just saying, give yourself some credit for even picking up a book like this. You're well on your way to creating healthy money patterns going forward.

Myth #5 – Credit cards are bad. Yes, this is a juicy myth. Credit cards, used wisely, make a great deal of sense. If you use, say, a points credit card like a debit card, charge your monthly expenses, and then pay them off every month, you get all the benefits without any downsides like high interest rates and debt. I've used credit card hacking to pay for trips and airfare with miles and points, and it's pretty nice. I would've spent the money anyway, but when I use a points credit card, I get something for the money I would be spending. We've already established that money is emotional, and if you don't have healthy spending patterns with credit cards, then maybe they aren't right for you now or ever. You have to be honest with yourself. It's okay to admit that having those little pieces of plastic in your wallet is just too much temptation. Take them out of your wallet. Disconnect your virtual wallet from your favorite online stores. Do what's in the best interest of your money goals. However you choose to interact with credit cards, that's your choice, not mine or anyone else's (unless they are financially dependent on you).

Myth # 6 – Being debt-free is always best. Yet another explosive topic with *sooooo* many opinions. Here's the way I think of it: Expensive debt, like credit card debt, can suck the life out of you. You want to pay that off ASAP. But you aren't a bad person if you have credit card debt. You might need a little help sorting out some money emotions and behaviors to create a motivational plan to pay off your balances. Nothing wrong with that. I'd argue that having a mortgage while you are in your working years and potentially getting a tax deduction can make sense. Student loan debt can also make sense, but I think you also need to consider the likelihood of paying it off in a reasonable amount of time. When I went to grad school, student loans were given out like candy. I didn't think about how much debt I would have; I was just focused on the degree. I could have chosen a much less expensive college and still gotten an MBA. You can't undo anything, but if you're thinking about going back to school, really check yourself and see if it makes sense to make the investment. The point is that debt can be soul-sucking, but it does not indicate the caliber of who you are.

Myth #7 – Every couple has to fight about money. I've helped many very happy couples who have never argued about money. I think the key is to be honest with each other, to share openly about what stresses you out around money, and to understand each other's money story from childhood. We all have a story and that story colors how we think, act, and feel about money. Your story is going to be unique to you. Offering a safe space for your partner to share is critical and a loving thing to do. We already do enough damage to ourselves by judging and shaming our money choices . . . we don't need a partner to pile on their judgment. So please, be gentle with each other.

I'm not encouraging you to turn into someone you've seen fictionalized in movies who is a money-loving, greedy fool. I hope you understand my approach in this chapter of welcoming in a sense of play and curiosity with your relationship with money. When you can visualize your relationship with money in the context of other relationships in your life, you can start to see some glaring red flags of negativity and neglect, which are certain ick factors. I want to help you remove as much ick as possible so you can keep money in check without steamrolling your emotions.

QUESTIONS TO PONDER

1. This question has nothing to do with money, but it's fun to ponder. What would a perfect date look like to you?
2. What are some of the money myths that you've believed to be true (but are ditching after this chapter)?
3. What does wealth mean to you? Can you quantify it?
4. For all you creatives out there, write a dating profile as if you were trying to attract your ideal relationship with money.

What's the Story of Your Money?

My Grandma Hilda was what you call these days a badass. She was born in rural northern Indiana in the early 1900s and was a female entrepreneur before it was trendy and common and when women's rights around money were limited (and that's putting it mildly). Most women could only dream of running a business, so when my grandma put the "open" sign on her home-operated beauty salon, it was a Big Deal.

It wasn't until 1963, when *The Equal Pay Act* was passed, that the promise of equitable wages for the same work regardless of race, color, religion, or sex of the worker was enacted. We've come a long way, but even currently, women still have to work *two and a half months* longer than men to earn the same amount of money. That's just 84 cents for every dollar a man earns, and for women of color, that number drops to 56 cents for every dollar. In 1974, The Equal Credit Opportunity Act was passed, which allowed women to open and create a credit application and get a loan without having a husband as a co-signer. This was the financial landscape that my grandma was living with, so I'm sure it would anger her – and many of our hard-working female ancestors – to know that even in the twenty-first century, we still have a long way to go.

All the women in and around her small town coveted my grandma's hair salon. Clients would come from miles away, sometimes from different states, to get a classic Hilda blowout and cut. She was quite the talker, too, so you always knew you were in for a good time with lots of gossip floating around the hair salon. (That is truly the mark of a good hair salon if you ask me.) Hilda worked tirelessly and actually became a bit of a workaholic for years to feed her family, put a roof over their heads, and escape some very real money trauma. Her motivation was simple: She never, ever wanted to run out of money. Never.

Grandma Hilda lived through the depths of the Great Depression. Although I never got to speak to her about her experiences before she passed away, I know that the reason she worked days, nights, weekends, and even holidays was because of the thought of having to stand in soup lines and ration food for a second time in her life was more than she could bear. That is something I can't even imagine having to live through. I'm very fortunate never to have to worry about having food to eat and clothes to wear. I realize this is quite a privilege, and I'm very grateful that on my list of worries, food, shelter, and clothing were never at the top.

When my grandma passed away in the 1980s, I was about five or six years old. When my dad went to clean out her house after her passing, he was in shock over the amount of frozen and canned food stored in every crevice of her home. It was enough to feed many families for weeks, if not months. You can't blame her, though. Having more than enough food was her way of dealing with the deeply woven fears of being unable to feed her family and herself. She was successful and made her own money, but that fear became a part of her identity, an imprint deep inside her. In fact, she never raised the prices for her hair salon clients. Many clients still paid the rate she charged when she opened her salon in the 1930s. I'm just guessing, but I wonder if she felt a certain responsibility to other families as well as hers to make sure each person always had enough money as well. Or, maybe she undervalued her worth because of the economic environment for women that she grew up in. How dare a woman make a financially prosperous living? I can't believe this is a part of our history as a country, but here we are. I have so many questions I would love to ask her.

Her husband, my grandfather, was one of the unlucky men during the Great Depression who did not have a job or, as a result, a source of income. The family relied entirely on my grandma and her hair salon business to meet their financial needs. Picture this: My grandma could start her business, earn money for the family, and become the sole provider for a very long time, but she couldn't get a credit card or loan without my grandfather co-signing. Now that's some unfair bullshit.

I thought of my grandma when I was sitting in that bank parking lot with a sense of panic, ready to look at my ATM receipt for the first time in many years. Her relationship with money was pretty messed up for good reason, but I can never know the depths of her despair and longing for dreams that would go unchecked. I wondered if she ever felt the same gut-wrenching fears around money that I was experiencing at that moment. Did she break out into a sweat when she was reconciling her bank account each month? Did she ever feel frozen when the topic of money came up? I wondered what advice she would give me at that moment. A stern, "Get it together, Shannah. You have more money than I ever dreamt of." Or would it be, "My heart aches for you, sweet girl, and I'm right here with you. I know how irrational and scary money is." I wonder what your grandma and her grandma and her grandma would say to you about your money fears, having walked through life during the Great Depression, racial inequities and slavery, immigrating to another country, and so many other impactful and terrorizing money moments. To some extent, we all carry those fears in our DNA. These fears become a part of our money story.

Grandma Hilda's money story is filled with success and struggle, pain and gratitude, and all of those themes have been passed down to me without me being consciously aware. Suddenly, my passive-aggressive unwillingness to stare at a bank receipt made a lot of sense. Maybe this fear didn't actually belong to me. Maybe these fears weren't just mine – they were also my parents', my grandparents', and other relatives I'd never met. If we look at some of the most impactful dates in history: The Great Depression from 1929 to 1939, The Great Inflation in the 1970s, the dot-com bubble burst in the late 1990s, the global financial crisis in 2008–2009, and more recently, the inflation surge from 2021 to 2023, it makes perfect sense why you might be carrying around a lot of gunk in your money story that's keeping you stuck without you even knowing it's there. This gunk translates into a complicated relationship with money (and that's putting it mildly). A stuckness factor that you can't seem to escape no matter how hard you try.

. . .

 MONEY TRUTH OR DARE

TRUTH: What's your favorite thing to spend money on that you will never give up?
DARE: Take five minutes and write down your biggest money regret, then tear up the piece of paper.

. . .

WHAT IS YOUR MONEY STORY?

You need to know this: Your money story started before you took your first breath. Your subconscious mind, which is formed between birth and age 7, is very powerful. It is estimated that 95% of your thoughts, feelings, and memories live there. Austrian neurologist Sigmund Freud said, "The mind is like an iceberg; it floats with one-seventh of its bulk above water" (https://www.simplypsychology.org/unconscious-mind .html). The part of your mind that floats underneath the water is your subconscious mind – and this part is vast and wide.

We typically have around 60,000 thoughts a day and most of them are thanks to our subconscious mind. Because this part of our mind impacts the majority of our thinking, we think, act, and feel based on our emotions. Your subconscious mind is like a giant memory bank storing information for years. Good thoughts, bad thoughts, and everything in between gets locked up here and influences your relationship with money. Your subconscious mind is always working in the background. Many money habits occur because of what's happening in your subconscious mind.

Between ages *2 and 6*, your critical and rational thinking is not significantly developed, so you tend to believe whatever you are told about life and money. "By age 3, your kids can grasp basic money concepts. By age 7, many of their money habits are set." (*Kobliner, PBS*) So, you *are* learning about money, but the key is, what are you learning about your *relationship* with money? Think back to those seemingly tame money comments that were made in your family, like, "Money doesn't grow on trees," "Bring home the bacon," or "Money is the root of all evil." These statements are absorbed by your subconscious mind, which then starts to develop beliefs about money that your body and brain think are real. Then, years later, you find yourself up for a pay raise and graciously decide not to ask for what you're worth because your subconscious mind believes money is the root of all evil and making more money isn't good for you. Or you get into credit card debt because money was tight as a kid and you felt deprived, so now as an adult you feel a sense of freedom whenever you buy something for yourself. Perhaps even you had a negative experience around money as a kid so now you're hyper-focused on saving as much money as you can and never getting into debt or taking any financial risks.

See how sneaky your money story and beliefs are? This is why it's so important to understand the story of your money and the history of money within your family unit. I get so mad when people say that the reason someone is in debt is because they are lazy, or someone just needs to take on more risk with their retirement funds and they could have millions saved. Money is just not this cut and dried. You can't just apply rational logic to the areas where you feel stuck financially.

. . .

 ## YOUR RELATIONSHIP WITH MONEY IS. . .

A conversation with Meghan Dwyer, Certified Financial Planner and host of the *Money Isn't Scary* podcast

Shannah: If you were to describe your relationship to money as a cartoon character, what would it be?

Meghan: This is such a great question. It's a two-piece answer for me. I would say my relationship with money used to be Charlie Brown. I always think of this because I just watched this episode with my kids recently, the Great Pumpkin Charlie Brown episode, where they're out trick or treating. All the other kids are saying "I got a lollipop; I got a chocolate." Charlie Brown says "I got a rock", and we laugh at that line in my house, but it's just so representative of this kind of victim mindset that we throw ourselves into and get into. I know for sure it's something that I've inherited in my family. But it doesn't feel good. It doesn't feel good to carry around a bag of rocks when you're out trick-or-treating. So, through a lot of the work I've done, my relationship with money is more Snoopy; it's more happy to be here, just enjoying it and going with the flow.

Shannah: What first thought comes to mind when you think about money?

Meghan: Money doesn't have to be scary. It's hard to remember that, even for me, as someone who helps people with their money.

. . .

THOSE MONEY BELIEFS

"Somehow, we've forgotten that money is one of those things that's impacted by our childhood, and often, if we take kind of a curious and compassionate lens to why we're doing what we're doing as adults, we can go back to those formative years and think through how we might be responding or behaving with money based on what we learned as children," shared Certified Financial Therapist Lindsay Bryan-Podvin. Often, we repeat patterns with money that we saw as children into adulthood without really understanding where those patterns originated. Lindsay points out, "You can have two people who grew up in the same household and received the same seeming messages about money who have completely different relationships with money because of how they interpreted the messages."

This is why you need to not only understand your money story but also how you interpret it – both are equally powerful and critical. For example, let's take two kids who grew up in the same household. They both heard their parents fight and argue about money all the time. One sibling might take that message and say to themselves, "Money is really stressful. I will have enough money never to have to worry about finances when I grow up." Maybe that sibling then goes off to college and gets a high-paying job, believing that the more money they make, the less stressful life will be. They work themself to the core, ignoring their health, sleep, and relationships. Money is their sole focus and they will do whatever it takes to make more than enough money. They may be well off financially, but are they living a well-lived life?

The other sibling sees money as something that causes frustration, anger, resentment, and more. Their motto is, "Money causes heartache, so I will do everything to avoid money. I will get into a career I love and follow my heart's passion." While they may love their career, their aversion to money could be so strong that they miss paying bills, don't plan to get out of student loan debt, or, like me, do not want to look at their bank account balance. They are happy with their life, but aren't financially well off.

Here, you've got two siblings who grew up in the same household but have different relationships with money based on their money story and how it resonated with them. If you have a sibling, can you see differences in how your money story and the interpretation of it have manifested differently between you and your sibling? There isn't a right or wrong interpretation. There's just your interpretation and how it impacts your relationship with money as an adult. This is where compassion comes into the equation. Compassion for your money journey and acceptance for someone else's. That is what you want to pay attention to.

Your money story is a mix of how you were raised, the verbal and nonverbal messages you received about money, and the truckload of false money beliefs you learned as a child. Nonverbal messages are just as important, if not more important, than verbal ones. If your family never talked about money, it's as crushing to your money beliefs as your family talking negatively about money. You learn that it is not okay to talk about money. You may feel ashamed about asking money questions you don't know the answer to. You might be uncomfortable around money. Either way, these messages influence your financial decisions as an adult.

This is why it is so critical to teach your kids about money from an early age. Little kids, even babies, are picking up money messages every single day. There are lots of expert opinions on what you should teach your kids about money and at what age. I tend to think the earlier you can get them involved in money decisions the better their relationship with money will be. For example, when a child is young, can they do a chore around the house, that's easy of course, and earn a little money? With that money, can you help them figure out what to spend it on? Maybe an ice cream, or donating it, or saving it for a friend's birthday gift. Another great idea is to get kids involved in deciding which family trips to take. You can sit down with them and share the budget that you have, and walk them through how much each trip will cost, and the activities you can do as a family with that budget. Once you're on the trip, you can have daily talks about budget decisions from food to activities and more. The mission is to get your kids comfortable talking about money and making intentional decisions. Have them help you figure out how to spend money. Adam Carroll, author of *The Build a Better Life Manifesto*, gave a TED Talk that has more than six million views about an experiment he played with his kids during a game of monopoly. Once they were playing with real money, his kids changed how they interacted with money. (It's fascinating, you need to watch it if you have kids.) They made more intentional choices. Money came to life.

Another piece of the puzzle is that your subconscious mind is where your behaviors, habits, patterns, and beliefs about money operate. This part of your mind also stores your fears, insecurities, memories, worries, and trauma about money. So, if you allow those negative thought patterns about money in your subconscious mind to go unchecked, they will take over and run the show.

 TRY THIS...

Understanding your money story is important in healing your relationship with money. To fully grasp the big picture, you need to see it before your eyes. I call this exercise the Money Timeline. It's a very simple exercise that allows you to spot patterns and beliefs that you have about money.

Take out a blank sheet of paper and draw a line down the center of the page. (I like to turn my page horizontally for this exercise so you have more room to write.) Draw a plus sign or write the word "Positive" at the top of the line and a negative sign or the word "Negative" at the bottom of the page. Starting with whichever side of the line resonates more with you, fill in important moments in your money story. You can write as much or as little detail as you'd like. For example, on the negative side of the line, you might have some instances such as taking college loans, having $5,000 of credit card debt, needing to pay $1,000 in car repairs, getting a divorce, having to move for your job to an expensive city, fighting with your partner about money, getting laid off or fired from a job, starting a business that didn't turn out to be profitable, taking out a loan to cover your monthly expenses, being a victim of identity theft or fraud, a decrease in your credit score because you missed a bill, etc. You could also add your feelings toward money on the negative side of the line if, for example, you felt constant dread or anxiety around money for a few years. Once you add the big moments, you can start filling in the smaller ones.

For the positive side – you guessed it – list all the good things that have happened with money in your life. For example, I got a big pay raise, paid off $75K of debt or student loans, traveled worldwide for a year and freelanced, launched a podcast, started my business, inherited money that I put to good use, started investing or grew my investments to $100K, bought a house, got six months maternity leave, wrote my book, etc.

When you are finished filling in the Money Timeline, circle the items you feel had a big impact on your money journey. Ask yourself, "How have these moments shaped my current relationship with money?" If you want extra credit, doing this exercise with your parents can be super-helpful. Or, if you don't feel comfortable talking to your parents about their money story, fill in as much detail as you can think of. Usually, you find similar money patterns between your parents and yourself. The situations might be different, but the patterns might be quite familiar. These patterns are clues to revealing the areas of your relationship with money that might need some healing or a deeper dive.

My friend Rebecca worked on the Money Timeline exercise when she was stuck trying to reach her goal of paying off $32K of debt that she had accumulated from college into her 30s. She'd always get close to paying off her credit cards, only to find herself charging more each month and getting back into debt. The interest Rebecca had paid over the years on her credit card debt was double the amount she still owed. She sat down one day with me and created her Money Timeline over a giant piece of white chocolate raspberry cheesecake and a cup of green tea. With every bite of cheesecake she ate, she'd think of something else to add to her timeline, like the time her car broke down on the side of the road; it cost her $350 to get towed and another $1,500 for repairs when she only had $200 left in her bank account, a moment that made her feel like reaching her money goal would always be out of her reach. She also recounted getting a big raise at work for 30% more than she had earned the previous five years, only to lose her job two weeks later without severance pay when the company closed. After that traumatic event, her credit cards became the only way she could pay her bills for a few months. She shamed and blamed herself every time she pulled out that piece of plastic and tapped it to pay for something she needed. Surely "she was failing at money" was the predominant thought pattern running through her head.

She thought about her parents' divorce when she was a teenager and how suddenly each parent was worried about money, so much so that she was convinced they would lose their house. Until that point, she and her sisters always had a birthday party with lots of gifts. Now, she was told she could pick out just one gift for her birthday, and it had to be under $50. Then, she considered the trip to New York City to see her favorite band and how she bought a watch she had always wanted. She could lend her sister money to start her business, and she paid for an expensive certification needed to advance her career. Bite by bite, her Money Timeline was exploding with detail.

Rebecca put her fork down and said, "Okay, I think I'm done. Now what?" She went through her cluttered Money Timeline and circled the big moments. She paused after each step, waiting for my further instructions. I asked her to write the name of her money story. If she had to pick one title, just like a movie title, as the name of her money story, what would that be? Rebecca pondered for a while, finishing the last bite of cheesecake. "Overwhelmed and Unprepared," she said. "I just feel like every time I get ahead of money, I fall back behind. Now, I can see that represented in my money story. When I make positive money advances, something rocks that boat, and I feel devastated. But I also see how I'm putting a lot of weight on the negative things that happen to me versus all the positive progress I have made," she shared. "On second thought, I don't want that to be the name of my money story going forward. Can I change the name to Surviving to Thriving?"

The Money Timeline reveals your past money story, thoughts, and those big moments that stand out to you. However, it's backward-looking because it only represents what has happened to you in the past. From this point forward, you get to decide how you view the money moments in your life and what your money story will look like. Could a negative money moment be something good in disguise? Could it be a teacher for defining a new relationship with money? Could these money moments be normalized as just a part of living life as a human? I encourage you to do this exercise and discuss it with your friends and family. Talking openly about money is a powerful mechanism to bring money out of the shadows and create a healthy future money story.

HOW COULD YOU, MONEY?

Game 5 of the Western Conference Finals with the Los Angeles Lakers versus the Phoenix Suns is a day I'll never forget. I had a hot-ticket seat at the Staples Center to see the action with 18,996 other excited fans. The score was close the entire game – one of those games where legends are made. All the regular stars were out that night – Jack Nicolson, Paula Abdul, Magic Johnson, and many other famous faces. With time running out, the Lakers scored the final basket and won the game 103–101 vs. the Suns. The crowd roared, my parents and I high-fived each other, and Randy Newman's classic song, "I Love L.A.," played loudly in the arena. I was on a proverbial high. That was until I received a call on the way home that would change my life.

"Hey, so I just got fired from my job and was told to pack my stuff and leave," my now ex-husband said. "Wait, what did you say?" I asked, hoping he'd say it was a joke or I had misunderstood. "I said I got fired, and I'm on my way home," he repeated. Right then and there, I felt the most intense feelings of panic and fear throughout my entire body. I wanted to run away quickly or hide under the covers in my bed and never come out. One of the best days ever had gone *poof* right before my eyes.

To this day, I feel a sense of immense life-threatening discomfort every Memorial Day weekend. It's like having a new shoe that's mercilessly rubbing open your heel when you're on a five-mile walk, and you have no choice but to continue to walk ahead. I remember the cloud of confusion around how we would pay our bills. We weren't exactly living above our means, but we needed to make some fast changes without two incomes, or we'd find ourselves in debt quickly. I was shocked at how I felt. It was as if someone had just taken away all my possessions and locked me up with no way out. I had trouble breathing and, in a couple of moments, swore I was having heart issues. I couldn't concentrate during conversations at home that weekend, so I watched every episode of my favorite show, *Parenthood*, on mute, wallowing in self-pity.

Remember, emotions around money are felt within your body as well as experienced externally. I didn't know it at the time when I was feeling so terrible. I also didn't realize that these negative and traumatic emotions around money can get stuck inside you and have lingering effects for years.

I had felt this money pain before, just a few years earlier, when my career came crashing down. I started a business in college, Hometown

Cinema, which was one of the first national student film festivals. It's one of my proudest achievements, besides my podcast, *Everyone's Talkin' Money*. I built the film festival up and partnered with an entertainment company run by a well-known Hollywood producer. That company even hired me to run their collegiate programming department while I ran the festival. The Cliff Notes version is that the company suffered the demise that many did with the internet bubble collapse in the early 2000s, and my income and film festival went down in one swoop. The night of the collapse, I joined my family for dinner at a Mexican restaurant, and while my body might've been there, my brain and emotions were swirling thinking about how devastating this news was to my career and my bank account. I ate two bites of a tortilla and sat silently the entire night. "Why aren't you saying anything tonight?" my dad asked in between bites of his tacos. I just stared blankly at him and smiled, "I don't know." But really, I did know, I just didn't know how to articulate what I was feeling. I believed that my career and the amount of money I made defined who I was as a person. I'm not sure I knew how to separate myself from my achievements. (To be honest, that is a money belief that I'm still working through.) Although it was years later, my body returned to this freeze mode it had rehearsed years before on that faded Memorial Day weekend.

Our options weren't great. We could drain his retirement savings and pay a hefty penalty and taxes on the money we withdrew. We could take out a loan, but how would we repay that? We could cut every expense necessary, but we'd still have to pay our mortgage, utilities, and car payments. Everywhere I looked, the options seemed painful and anxiety-filled.

I stared at the wall all weekend long painstakingly searching my brain for ideas of how we would pay for our bills. I'm an over-thinker and was having trouble thinking my way out of this situation. Here were a few things I came up with to try and stem the bleeding:

1. Figured out what expenses we could cut out or pause ASAP – things like our gym memberships and expensive dinners out on a whim.

2. Called our credit card companies and asked for an interest rate reduction and requested that they waive our annual fees. (Yes, you can do this, and it's successful a lot of the time. You just have to ask the questions.)

3. Called our cell phone and internet companies and found out there was a better plan we could move to that saved us, in total, $105 a month.

4. Did the math and figured out if we took out $25K from our retirement plan, we could at least pay all our bills for six months with a little left over to cover the taxes.

5. Got serious about shopping smarter at the grocery store and meal planning. How could we make three meals out of what we bought? I got creative and watched every episode of The Food Network's show *Everyday Italian* with Giada De Laurentiis.

6. Did my best to try not to panic. (Not successfully, I'll report.)

I didn't grow up having to worry about money, and I know that is a huge privilege. What I couldn't understand, though, was why I felt a sense of trauma about not being able to pay our bills. This wasn't entirely rational for me. Where did it come from? I had always been able to pay my bills, even when I had credit card debt from my college days and very little income. My subconscious mind worked in overdrive to sort through all those money-related beliefs formed when I was young. And the biggest of those beliefs I didn't realize I held? Not being able to pay my bills would make me appear like a failure. A failure to my friends and, most importantly, to my family, whose opinion I highly valued. Having to borrow money or ask for financial help felt excruciating. Again, who am I as a person if I don't have enough money to pay for things?

WHY DOES MONEY STRESS ME OUT?

Money stress doesn't just belong to me. The most common question I'm asked time and time again is, "Why does money always stress me out?" I will be bold and say that almost every human breathing on this earth feels some stress around money. I've spent years trying to get to the bottom of money stress and why it seems a part of the human experience. You could be walking into your favorite local pizza joint where the pizza tastes like pure heaven, meeting some of your best friends for a weekly hangout meal when suddenly there it is . . . money stress. Your chest tightens. Your brain can't think of anything but the bills in your inbox that need to be paid. "This is my happy place; why in the world am I anxious about money right now?" you growl to yourself. Your brain will work on autopilot around money unless you give it a new direction. This is the part that takes work.

Your brain is very lazy. It likes comfortable patterns, even if those patterns are destructive. I think this is one of the main reasons why making changes with your money decisions is so very difficult. Your brain likes to tell the same story about money. Your body just goes along for the ride. If I asked you, "What is your central money theme or thought that plays on repeat in your head," what would you tell me? A common theme I hear a lot is, "I've made really good money, but I don't have a lot to show from it. It's so embarrassing to even talk about." My follow-up question is, "What does it mean to not have a lot to show from it? How are you defining what 'a lot' means?" My central money thought is, you really should've made better money choices years ago. Yes, not a constructive statement and one that has me convinced I'm just doomed to make bad choices. See, we all have these stories that go on in the back of our minds, unrehearsed, on autopilot. They aren't helpful, most of the time. In fact, some of our stories are so negative that if we had to voice them out loud, we'd feel very awkward doing so.

Once you realize your central money thought or theme, the next step is to interrupt it. I've got a few tools you can borrow in those moments. The first step is noticing you are in an unhealthy pattern of thinking, likely there from your childhood years. The second step is to allow that thought to be there. Don't try to force it away. It's okay to feel this feeling. Next, you want to create a moment of pause and ask yourself this question. In these moments when you're noticing this repetitive money thought, how can you make a different choice in your thought pattern or with a current money decision? For example, let's say your thought pattern is that you've made too many mistakes and you're convinced that is what you'll do going forward, so you say goodbye to your goals and go spend $100 on dinner. A new approach going forward in those moments is to take a pause, feel your feelings, and then reassess your action. Do you really want to go to dinner or are you just trying to cover up a feeling that you might need to just sit in? Is that dinner worth it, or would your money be better spent toward a money goal? You are negotiating with yourself in these moments, but from a place of mindful thinking and being present. You are in control, not your money or your emotions.

Another great trick to try is grabbing a mason jar or some other container and labeling it, "good money thoughts." Write out some new healthy money thoughts you can reach for when those nasty lazy money thoughts come up. Fill this jar with as many thoughts as you'd like and keep it in a place you can easily access it. When you choose a new thought, let it sink in for a moment. Your brain might instantly say, "Oh, yeah, you don't *really* believe this good thought, do you?" Your job is to reply, "I'm working on it, so I'm going to try it on for a while. Why don't you just quiet down."

Here are some thoughts you can borrow, if you'd like:

- I'm making good choices with my money today
- I love myself and my money choices
- I'm happy with the place I'm at in life and don't need to change anything
- My past doesn't represent my future
- I can have an emotional day and still make intentional money choices
- The more money I make, the more people I can help
- My money situation does not define me

. . .

 UNRAVELING THOUGHT #3

The question isn't why money stresses you out. The question is, what are you really so stressed about and why? That's where the story of your money plays out.

. . .

We've already talked about this: Your relationship with money is tangled up. You know that dread you feel in your chest when you look at your bank account balance or that feeling of complete panic when some unexpected expense comes up that you were wholly unprepared for? Yes, that's money showing up at your door telling you your relationship needs some good TLC. The good news is that you aren't alone.

Stress related to money and inflation is at the highest level *recorded since 2015*. Ask any therapist, and they will tell you that money is also one of the leading causes of divorce here in America. It makes sense. The reason why your relationship with money is so messed up is not that you took out that credit card in college in exchange for a very bad T-shirt bearing the credit card company's logo that swiftly found its way into the trash can. It's messed up because we live in a society that somehow puts learning about Medieval History above learning about the ins and outs of money – something inescapable and a primal need we all share. As if that isn't enough, classic money books don't help. Most books you find on the bookshelf give a long list of money how-tos like budgeting, saving, and investing, but leave out one critical piece of information – what's going on in the background that's stopping you from achieving your money goals. This is your money story, and it's the biggest reason money stays a nemesis in your life. Your money story dictates how you think, act, and feel about money.

Don't believe me? Be honest with yourself. On a scale of 1–5, with five being seriously messed up, and one being minorly messed up, how messed up would you say your relationship with money is?

Your reasons may be many and varied; none of them are inherently your fault. These include false family-centered money beliefs, generational money beliefs, money trauma (big and small), shame, guilt, self-esteem, and so much more. The things you do learn about money from an early age are subconscious biases and beliefs that become rooted in your thinking and impact your thoughts, feelings, and actions around money. These beliefs from childhood can form money blocks or blind spots in how you interact with money. Uncovering your story helps you unravel the *how* and *why* behind your current relationship with money. It can help you remove your money blocks and, for the first time, create a path toward your money goals and a life well-lived, whatever that looks like for you.

You can change your money story going forward. Why not start now?

QUESTIONS TO PONDER

1. What big money moments stand out in your life thus far?
2. What money messages did you receive as a child?
3. What was your parents'/grandparents' relationship with money like?
4. How many times do you think about money every day? What are those thoughts telling you?

CHAPTER 4

What's Your Money Trauma?

A forceful knock at your door one morning catches you off guard. You just finished pouring yourself a nice hot cup of coffee and are deeply offended that someone is pulling you away from this moment of bliss. You walk slowly to the door, turn the knob and answer, only to find money staring back at you. "Hey, how you doing? Can I come in and muck some stuff up and give you a lot more anxiety than you already have? I'll take a coffee, too."

If this actually happened to you, what would your visual representation of money look like? What would money say to you? Somehow, I've always thought my money would look like an older white man, say early 60s, with gray hair, and a pretty bad version of a comb-over, wearing some buttoned-up shirt, an uncoordinated tie, and loafers. It would be slightly pudgy with a completely disapproving look on its face, and have the worst bad breath.

This visual version of what money would look like and say to me stems from my belief that I will never be good enough to earn and accumulate money like an older white guy. I'll always be a bit behind and never be able to catch up, no matter how hard I try. I believe that money requires me to be perfect, but somehow, even the most disheveled male will always be better with their money than I will be. I am honestly so exhausted from having this belief about money that I'd love to stand on the tallest building and swing this belief off the ledge to fall to its death for all of us. Why do we believe that *everyone* is better at money than we are? I would like to talk back to money and tell it what I think of it using the choicest of four-letter words. I'm downright angry with money and its role in my life. It needs to go and pester someone else, because I've had it up to my ears. I'm tired of money causing divides between people and keeping good, hard-working people down. I'm angry that you need a lot of money to stay at a luxurious place and travel in first class. Don't we all deserve a bit of luxury, a top-shelf margarita with a fancy straw and decorative umbrella from time to time and, for God's sake, a lay-flat seat when we fly?

I'd say, what is it with you, money? Why do you insist on torturing us out here just trying to make it through life? You don't care if we have a lot of money in our bank account or a little; you're determined to impose some pain at some point in our lives. I really hope you have something to say for yourself, money. Oh, and don't get me started on the whole perfectionism stance. Can we just call it a truce and agree that perfectionism is seriously messing us all up?

Perfectionism is one of the most common causes of money trauma (yes, I used that word), and it's something that is universally felt. You're probably nodding your head, but here's the headline you never see: There is no such thing as perfect regarding your money, and you will make mistakes! And you will make those mistakes repeatedly because you are human. Can you tell me what being perfect with money even looks like? Right, that's what I thought. It doesn't exist, so why do we all cling so tightly to that gravitational pull? What would it look like to give yourself permission to make money mistakes without an ounce of judgment? It's a pretty freeing thought to ponder. Perhaps, by the end of this journey, we can all agree to tell money to shove it. Or preferably, agree to a mutual friendship that is supportive for both parties.

WHAT IS MONEY TRAUMA?

Money is one of the most significant trauma bonds in someone's life, and it's sneaky. Trauma is not just what happens to you, but it's also about what happens inside you. It shapes your beliefs about you and your money. Trauma can be acute, which occurs just once; chronic, which happens over time; or complex, which is a horrifying mix of acute and chronic situations. Money trauma can be big, like losing your house or your job, or something small, such as a seemingly innocent money mistake you made or forgetting to pay a bill on time. What makes this traumatic is how you internalize it and the thoughts and feelings it evokes.

Trauma is stored in the limbic system, where our senses are experienced. This system controls emotions, behaviors, and fight-or-flight responses and is involved in emotional processing. So, in essence, money trauma is imprinted into you. People suffering from money trauma have behavior grounded in denial and avoidance that isn't rational or by choice, yet results in an increased inability to plan, organize, and manage one's financial life while simultaneously experiencing a full range of symptoms associated with post-traumatic stress disorder (PTSD). PTSD-like symptoms that can show up with money trauma include agitation, irritability, hypervigilance, self-destructive behavior, and isolation that can even lead to an inability to have loving feelings toward others. Money trauma isn't a specific diagnosis, though, unfortunately. There's still a lot of work to be done to start recognizing money trauma for what it is – traumatic.

Money trauma keeps you stuck. Think of it like quicksand. Keisha Blair, an economist who founded the Institute of Holistic Wealth, the *Holistic Wealth* podcast, and is widely regarded as The Mother of Holistic Wealth, believes that unresolved money trauma is a big reason you get stymied trying to reach your goals and can never feel at ease around money. "Unresolved money trauma can lead to millions of dollars in losses and unrealized potential over a lifetime (it can range on a scale from a severe gambling addiction with losses in the tens of millions of dollars to just paralysis with money). Some people will never realize their life purpose or full potential because of unresolved money trauma. It's like not knowing your identity. If we look at Maslow's hierarchy of needs and self-actualization, it occurs when we have a firm sense of our identity. Can you imagine not having a firm sense of your personal financial identity? It's hard to have financial self-actualization. Unresolved money trauma can lead to paralysis around investments, entrepreneurship, and a total lack of confidence around money. It can lead to highly addictive behaviors, overthinking, anxiety, depression, suicide, and questioning every money decision. It's difficult, if not impossible, to have full self-actualization if you have unresolved money trauma – it means you have not attained financial self-actualization. It's difficult to achieve your life's purpose with unresolved money trauma."

Money trauma can easily stem from money mistakes you feel deeply ashamed about; however, I need you to know that your money mistakes aren't original. We've all made the same stupid money mistakes, largely because there is a deep emotional connection behind your money decisions, and you don't have the tools in the toolkit to process them. You let your money story – that pesky, often negative and irrational narrative that is playing in your mind on a chronic loop – dictate your relationship with money. You keep quiet. You don't ask questions. You believe your worst money thoughts. So, your money mistakes start to define who you are and impact your self-image.

Have you ever made one of these mistakes?

- Taking on too much debt
- Making an investment decision that took a faceplant
- Swearing to save money only to spend it before it even reaches your savings account
- Buying something you saw on a social media post because "everyone else" is buying it
- Living paycheck-to-paycheck, always
- Lending your bff money when you know it will never get paid back
- Taking that soul-crushing job that you knew you would hate because the money is good
- Taking on too much student loan debt
- Not advocating for yourself at work and asking for more money
- Having a credit score dip
- Judging others about how they spend and save their money
- Not having very necessary conversations about money with your partner
- Spending your emergency fund on a vacation with your partner that you don't talk to anymore
- Stuck believing false money lies, like your self-worth = your net worth

I should also add buying a ridiculously expensive SUV that I should've never bought to the list because I have a deep sense of shame and trauma from making spending purchases that I knew were not good for my bank account.

These are just a few common money mistakes we all make. Mistakes are one thing, but not feeling like you have room to talk about them with anyone or ask questions to learn how to improve is what can lead to anxiety, shame, guilt, regret, and judgment. These emotions work to perpetuate mistakes; the cycle continues, and your trauma bond continues to grow.

. . .

 UNRAVELING THOUGHT #4

Here is a healthy way to look at mistakes. I made a mistake; great. I can learn what I need to do to avoid making a mistake again or understand WHY I made this mistake. I permit myself to make mistakes without shame, failure, or regret!

. . .

Want to know the secret to telling your brain that mistakes are okay? You recognize the mistake and then work to reframe it. Your brain creates templates of how to do things, and even though it might be classified as a mistake, like going over budget each month, it's a template, and it's what your brain knows to do. Ultimately, your brain is lazy, really lazy, and that's not your fault; it's how the brain was made. And your brain loves these comfy places that feel so familiar. So, instead of hyper-focusing on your mistake, try telling yourself that going over budget doesn't mean you are bad with money. It means you need to make some tweaks and figure out a better system for you. Insert whatever positive statement feels good to you at the moment, but don't let yourself stay stuck in the negative for too long. One of my favorite questions to ask is, "What if you could get a do-over for a money mistake?" Of course, you can't go backward, but what you can do is change your thoughts and actions going forward.

. . .

 MONEY TRUTH OR DARE

TRUTH: When or where do you spend the most amount of money?
DARE: Write down the interest rates for all your debts.

. . .

WHAT DOES MONEY TRAUMA LOOK LIKE?

Money trauma is sneaky. It's easy to think, "There's no way I have money trauma. I'm just stressed about money." However, the more hyper-focused you are on a topic, such as an avoidance to spend money or a need to spend money, tensing up when someone talks about money, avoiding asking for a pay raise or waking up in the middle of the night with racing thoughts about money, the more likelihood that some form of money trauma exists. Asking yourself, "How do I feel about money?" is a great starting point to uncover your money trauma.

The first step to unraveling money trauma is to notice what's happening in your body around money. For example, do you get stressed on payday and have neck soreness or a racing heart? When around certain people, do you get fearful or shut down when anything related to money comes up? Does your voice get higher-pitched when talking about money? Do you hate looking at your bank account balance? Do you feel scared when you're negotiating for a higher salary?

Unresolved money trauma creates nervous system dysregulation within the body and can manifest in anger, anxiety, isolation, depression, and defensiveness.

Money trauma often looks like this:

- Overspending: If you are nervous or triggered by money, you might overspend to get a chemical response to feel better. Also, if you grew up financially insecure, you might tend to overspend because you aren't used to having money readily available. Overspending from time to time is normal and something we all partake in. It feels good to spend money, and I encourage you to do so in healthy doses. If you find yourself chronically overspending, however, that's the signal to explore what form of trauma might be present. Explore where your need to overspend comes from.

- Avoidance: You tend to avoid looking at your money or talking about money. In a relationship, you often avoid discussing money with your partner because you fear shame or judgment. Again, a healthy dose of avoidance is common and normal. Most of us don't really enjoy talking about money. However, if you find yourself resonating with my story of never looking at my ATM receipts, that is for sure a sign of money trauma. Ask yourself, what am I fearing the most.

- Codependent behavior: You're capable of making money, but you rely on someone to take care of all the money-related activities, including earning it, out of fear. Now, I'm not talking about consciously deciding for a family that one partner works and the other stays home. Codependent behavior involves purposefully avoiding money-related activities. This is a sign of money trauma. What are you getting from being codependent (or avoiding)?

- Not spending money: You hold onto money or are super-conservative because you fear money might run out, or you want to be prepared "just in case" anything bad happens. Not spending money is certainly not a bad money trait. What you want to watch out for is being conservative with your money to a fault. Not spending money on things that would bring you joy or furthering your wealth accumulation. This is another sign of money trauma. What is at the root of not wanting to spend money?

– – – – –

The unthinkable happened to my friend, Carey. She was at home, elbow deep in suds, bathing her young child, when she realized she hadn't seen or heard from her fiancé in quite a while. Something didn't seem right, so she wrapped her child in a towel and walked around the house to find her fiancé. She searched every room, opening doors and turning on lights. Nervous energy started to race through her body. Where was he? Tragically, she found him lying on the floor, blood-stained, with a gun next to him. The horror was magnified by this tiny life she held in her arms, witnessing their father's passing. The feelings were simply too intense to deal with at the time.

Unknowingly to Carey, her fiancé had purchased a life insurance policy but forgot to list her as the beneficiary. She was living in an expensive house they had recently bought, with a small child and little income to support them going forward. "How am I going to afford to live when I can't even process what just happened?" she begged for an answer. "I don't know, but we'll figure it out," was the best I could muster. Carey's story might be an extreme example of money trauma, but my guess is you have experienced some form of money trauma in your life, perhaps without you even knowing it exists.

Money trauma can come from anywhere:

- Survivor's guilt from receiving life insurance money. This is often referred to as blood money. The trauma of losing a loved one can create feelings of guilt when you receive a life insurance death benefit.

- Poverty

- Homelessness

- Food insecurity

- Unemployment due to being fired or laid off (don't underestimate this one)

- Financial abuse from a partner

- Racism

- Marginalization

- Sexism

- False belief systems about money

- Generational money patterns

- Increasing debt and inflation

- Financial discrimination, especially for women and women of color

- Lack of financial resources. The feeling of being alone trying to figure it all out and not having access to financial literacy information.

- Feeling unworthy and stuck ruminating about money mistakes you've made

There are also behavioral signs of money trauma, such as gambling, hoarding, financial denial, impulsively spending any sudden windfalls, and repeated poor money decisions.

Understanding your money trauma can help you heal your relationship with money and provide a pathway to move closer to your money goals. It is nearly impossible to think clearly and make mindful money decisions when you are stuck in patterns of trauma or shame around money. It is common to develop PTSD-like symptoms as well that can lead to fight or flight, freeze, or fawning actions. I'm a freezer for sure. I like to avoid conflict at all costs, even when it comes to my money.

Start by asking yourself some questions like:

Why do I overspend?

Why do I accumulate debt?

Why do I get stuck in repetitive patterns?

Why do I avoid dealing with my money?

Why am I not charging what I'm worth?

Why can't I seem to save money?

Why am I afraid to spend money?

Why do I get angry when I talk about money with my partner?

These questions won't fix your money trauma. But if you're honest with yourself, you can get to the root of your money beliefs and understand why you do or don't perform certain actions when it comes to money. This is the basis for creating the changes you want with your money.

SYSTEMIC MONEY TRAUMA

I would be remiss if I left out of the conversation the systemic money issues that might be getting in the way of you being able to achieve financial success. Systemic inequities and barriers keep people of color from financial security and financial freedom through the lack of education and homeownership. This results in decreased wealth and income.

These include:

1. Pay gap and low wages, especially if you are BIPOC
2. Lack of financial literacy and access to education
3. The cost of college in the United States and student loan debt
4. Medical debt, which is the leading cause of bankruptcy

5. Access to affordable healthcare
6. Institutional or governmental policies and laws
7. Systemic poverty and homelessness
8. Redlining and denying people access to credit and home loans depending on where they live

Homeownership has been one of the most effective ways in the United States that have kept people of color from building wealth that can be passed down from generation to generation. People of color applying for mortgage loans face a likelihood of being denied compared to white applications.

How can you get ahead when the "system" won't let you? Paco De Leon, author of the book *Finance for the People,* has something to say about the systemic and societal money issues that get in the way of reaching money goals and, ultimately, cause money trauma. "Let's look at earning money. The wage gap has a real impact on how much money folks from marginalized communities earn. This, in turn, impacts how much one can save and invest. The results of not earning enough aren't just seen on someone's bank account and balance sheet. Not earning enough will put someone in a state of chronic stress. This state inhibits good financial decision-making, which can then create a cycle of less-than-ideal financial decisions that lead to less-than-ideal outcomes. It's a vicious cycle. Personally, my own sense of self-worth is something I've had to spend lots of time, energy, and money on rebuilding. So much of my lack of self-worth was an internalization of society's idea of my worth (or lack thereof). Everyone will have their own unique struggle in life; it's part of the human experience. I think once you recognize that's a given in life, you can start to find ways to exercise your power in the face of circumstances outside of your control."

These systemic forms of money trauma are hard to overcome, especially if they have existed for generations before you. That's why the first step toward healing is to bring awareness to any generational money trauma in your family line. Uncovering the trauma bonds will help you see how you might be repeating patterns in your relationship with money. The second step is acceptance of what was. You can't change the past or any money trauma you have experienced to this point. You can change the future, though, which brings you to the third step: action.

HOW DO YOU HEAL?

Healing starts with understanding your money story and the factors that play into your trauma response. Recall how you were raised, and what money patterns are repeated automatically from childhood. Think about how your parents talked about or didn't talk about money. Were there any relationships you were in where you felt financial discomfort? Money trauma isn't a sign of weakness and doesn't mean you can't cultivate a healthy relationship with money going forward.

These waters are tricky to navigate, and I recommend talking to a therapist or a financial therapist to help give you an outside perspective and work through your thoughts and feelings around money. Because money is such a primal need, it's easy not to want to talk about your mistakes and explore these areas of trauma; however, doing so will help you begin to build a healthy relationship with money.

▶ TRY THIS...

Here are some other ways you can start to heal money trauma. Pick one or two to try out, and go slow. Money trauma is not created overnight, and neither will the healing process be remedied in a short period of time.

1. Journaling is a great way to explore your relationship with money in a safe space. Writing yourself a "Hey, Money" letter daily is a good exercise. Humanize money and write to it to tell it how you feel, what you're struggling with, and so on. You can also create an unstructured journal by exploring many of the prompts in this chapter. If journaling isn't your thing, why not take a more artistic approach and write a poem about your feelings about money or create a song? You can adapt this idea to fit your personality.

2. Self-care is critical to healing. Find ways to calm your nervous system, like getting out in nature for a walk, doing yoga, or listening to meditations. Lean back into the hobbies you enjoyed as a child, like coloring, putting a puzzle together, or dancing. Be gentle with yourself as you work on your relationship with money.

3. Create moments of pause. If you tend to overspend, create a boundary like my 24-hour spending pause. Put everything you want to buy in your online shopping cart, and then wait 24 hours before you hit the buy-now button. When

you return to the shopping cart in 24 hours, you won't even want or need half of the items you put in the cart. This is my go-to method to avoid overspending online. I get a rush just putting everything into my cart, and then I feel pretty proud of myself when I start taking things out of the cart the next day.

4. Talk to a friend, family member, or partner about your money worries. Make sure this person is trusted and will not shame or judge you. This is *very* important. Talking about money can help you see how you relate to others and that we are all more alike than we know when it comes to money fears and worries. I bet you when you share, your trusted friend or family member might have experienced some of the same feelings. Think of it as a bonding exercise.

5. Set money boundaries with others. If you've been helping your family members with their monthly bills because you feel responsible, set a boundary where you tell them you can only financially commit to a certain amount of money or you will help them for a specific time. Taking this step does not make you a bad person. You might feel a bit uncomfortable during the process, but that is okay. You are redefining their relationship with money in the process.

6. Regular and frequent self-check-ins are important. Dig into your thoughts and feelings about money each day. These check-ins are reminders to calm your nervous system if you're feeling triggered. In addition, asking yourself questions like, "Do I need to worry about this now?" or "Is there an action I can take today that is healthy for me?" are great ways to offer yourself some money TLC.

Our brains also have a great ability to adapt and change. This is called neuroplasticity. Our brains can literally create new pathways and form new habits if we spend enough time retraining them. Therefore, repetition is key to healing your money trauma and forming a new relationship with money. It is estimated that it takes the brain three to six months to create new behavior patterns and form new habits. Don't worry if working through your money trauma feels like you're initially pushing a giant boulder uphill. It will get easier the more you unravel these trauma bonds and let go of shame. You can look for some of these signs as indicators that you are in the healing process.

You become more connected to your authentic self and your truth

You start setting healthy money boundaries with yourself and your loved ones

You're learning to train yourself how to think about money (with good thoughts)

You see how your emotions impact your body and take steps to de-stress

You are honoring your money choices rather than shaming yourself

. . .

 YOUR RELATIONSHIP WITH MONEY IS. . .

A conversation with Jordan Grumet, aka Doc G., the *Earn & Invest* podcast host and author of *Taking Stock*

Shannah: Tell me, how do you feel about money?

Jordan: I have a rocky relationship with money. At times when I was struggling with my career, I have thought it was the most important thing in the world. I saw it as a life-saving escape hatch. At other times, I have seen it as a great hindrance. As a set of malicious claws pulling me away from doing things I wanted and being the person I thought I could become. During these times the mirage of wealth clouded my vision and convinced me that the attainment of money far outweighed much deeper and more important activities. I now see money for what it simply is. A great tool, among many other tools, that we can use to live the life we want to live. No more . . . no less.

Shannah: What's one money mistake you wish you could get a do-over for?

Jordan: I think my biggest mistake has always been placing too much importance on money. I think it became a driving force in my life apart from what it could actually do for me. I was very clear on what my net worth should be, but I had no idea what that net worth would actually do for me. In the great GPS of life I mistook the highways and the byways for the destination. Only with wisdom have I realized that if you don't know what address to plug into your GPS in the first place, the technology (the money) doesn't truly serve you.

. . .

One of my greatest achievements as a money expert was teaching more than 5,000 first-generation students Financial Literacy during my 10 years at California State University Northridge. When I was approached to teach these classes, I sat back and thought about what the 18-year-old version of myself should have learned about money in college. We didn't use books; instead, we leaned on blogs, articles, podcasts, and YouTube videos to learn how money really worked. I wanted my students to understand how to use their money to create a supportive financial future intentionally.

Celia was a bright-eyed, 19-year-old first-generation student who had never learned anything about money when she came to my class. She was also six months pregnant and on her own to raise her child.

She worked at a small local store and made just above minimum wage. "Professor Shannah, I've got to figure this money thing out because I'm all I have," she told me one day after class with tears in her eyes. She pulled out her phone, went to her banking app, and passed the phone to me. Over the next few hours, we looked at her numbers, dove into her money story, talked about how money trauma impacts her, figured out what was important to her, and started to put the money pieces together. Celia was so proud of herself that she went home and taught her parents and her siblings about credit scores, the ins and outs of creating a spending plan, how to pay off debt, and why money is so emotional.

Two years later, Celia returned to visit me in that same classroom with her baby boy beside her. Her words still give me a sense of great achievement. "Professor Shannah, my family came from poverty and nothingness. We've been written off and overlooked. My parents did their best, but we often didn't have enough food. I was fortunate enough to get a scholarship to school, and I'm so glad I did. What you taught me saved my life and my child's life. The biggest lesson you taught me was how to be intentional with my money and look beyond where I came from to see where I could go. I also worked on my money beliefs and know that I deserve to be financially secure. I owe my relationship with money to you. I'm the first person in my family to get a degree, make a decent wage, own a car outright, and have a good credit score. I'm the first family member to break the chains of financial trauma and create a new story with money."

I wish I had learned about the role money trauma played in my life when I was Celia's age. I didn't understand why I felt certain emotions around money that didn't make sense. Why did I feel the need to overspend to try to impress other people? Ultimately, they didn't care whether I had a new outfit or a shiny car. Learning to value myself just as I am is still my journey. I'm still peeling back layers of my money-trauma onion so I don't repeat money patterns from my past. It's hard work, for sure. Give yourself a big bear-hug and trust that the hard work will pay off.

MONEY TRAUMA AND YOUR BODY

Shinzen Young, a famous mindfulness teacher, came up with an equation that demonstrates that what we resist, persists. Shinzen says

Suffering = Pain × Resistance. What if you didn't have to resist money trauma any longer and instead could let it be your teacher? When you're in a moment of trauma, your subconscious mind takes a snapshot, and the image and feeling stay within your body. Your body relives it when certain triggers occur, so your brain continues to perceive that your trauma is happening right now, even if it's not. Are you beginning to see why money is the leading cause of stress? If you keep your trauma unresolved, it sits in your nervous system and can cause disruptions like aggression, depression, anxiety, isolation, negativity, hypervigilance, sleep disruptions, chronic thinking, physical symptoms like a tight jaw, neck, and shoulders, and obsessive money thoughts.

Applying some money techniques can help you move through trauma, and I've got a bunch to put in your toolkit, including one of my favorites, writing a "What If" list. This list helps you figure out what really is the worst-case scenario and is it so bad after all. For example, if you fear that you might lose your job and it could result in trauma, your What If list might look like this:

What if I lose my job?

Did I really like this job?

What is it that I really wanted to do?

Is there something else I want to try?

What steps can I take today to set myself up for a better outcome?

Asking questions is very powerful, so I'll continue asking them throughout this book. Start with the above example to help you work through the core of what you're really worried about. That knowledge will put you in a powerful position to know how to work through and deal with money trauma. And I hope, when you find your answers, that you can unravel money trauma and let it fade off into the wind.

If reading this entire chapter has been scarier than watching *Scream* for the umpteenth time, here's what I want you to remember:

We all have money trauma.

You can heal from money trauma.

The first step is being aware of your money trauma and then accepting it for what it is.

You can face your money fears and survive, I promise. Just start by taking a tiny step in one direction.

QUESTIONS TO PONDER

1. Where do you feel money anxiety in your body? Can you recognize it while it's happening?
2. Have you suffered from money trauma? Can you identify it?
3. Have there been any systemic money issues that have held you back?
4. Can you take 15 minutes today and do something that makes you feel good? (Go for a walk, do yoga, take a bath, dance to your favorite song, pet your dog, etc.)

PART
II

How Can You Unravel Your Relationship with Money?

CHAPTER **5**

What's Your Money Identity?

Being raised by my mom, Cindy, was a privilege that I never take for granted. Think Carol Brady from the Brady Bunch crossed with Betty Crocker with a dash of Julia Child's sass. If you ever met Cindy, you instantly became one of her "adopted" children. She would put you on her text chain, send you loving Facebook messages, and pray endlessly for you as if you were one of her own. Growing up, I always thought everyone had a mom like mine. (If you didn't, just know you can borrow Cindy whenever you need a mom.)

Cindy is smart and witty, fiery, sweet, and to this day, will not go out of her house without a deep shade of coral on her lips, a few swipes of pale pink blush on her cheeks, and a perfectly manicured hairstyle. I cross every finger and toe, hoping I look as amazing as Cindy does as I age. (I value my mom too much to divulge her true age here, but let's just say she looks amazing for her age.)

When I was little, my mom would gently wake me up in the morning, "Shannah, rise and shine. It's time to get up and start the day," and then head downstairs to cook a delicious and filling breakfast before school. Scrambled eggs with ketchup were the usual request from my brother and me. If I was lucky, I'd get to hold the metal whisk with the handle that turned to combine the eggs with the milk before they hit the skillet. She'd oversee my efforts, always offering an upbeat vote of confidence. "Look at those amazing scrambled eggs you made. Good job," she'd say, always evoking a smile on my face. I felt like a champ those days when I made perfectly fluffy scrambled eggs. After breakfast, she'd put the finishing touches on our gourmet-style lunches and pack them neatly into our lunch boxes. Strawberry Shortcake and Wonder Woman were my go-to lunch boxes. I'm a child of the seventies, after all.

I became known as the girl with the most tasty lunches in school. I'd orchestrate trades before lunch with my friends. I'll give you half of my delicious chicken sandwich if you give me four squares from your chocolate bar. Some days, I wouldn't eat my lunch at all and instead negotiate trades to fulfill my never-ending sweet tooth. I can't begin to tell you how many Reese's Peanut Butter Cups I've eaten from lunch trades. Depending on the day, Cindy would drive me or walk with me to school and escort me home every day, asking how my day was and chatting about what we would do when school was over. "I want to go swimming," was my usual response, and if you've ever been to Houston, Texas, you understand. There's not much else you can do in that heat and humidity other than get in a pool of water or head straight for air conditioning. I'm still thankful I didn't have to pay those massive summer electric bills. Sorry, mom and dad. I'm still not sure how you did it.

My mom always volunteered at school and would make the most delicious baked goods that would wow all the teachers. She makes a mean chocolate chip Toll House–style cookie with a slightly gooey center and a crisp outer crunch, in case you were wondering. However, in between the cookies and amazing lunches, I was picking up money messages that would shape my money identity as an adult. When we'd go out clothes shopping, I'd watch my mom make a beeline for the Sale and Clearance racks that were usually hidden in the back of the store. I remember walking past aisles of clothes that were all beautifully styled, but I knew I'd need to wait until those went on sale to have a shot at wearing them. Buying clothes on sale became a bit of a game. "Oh, this one is 50% off and then an additional 20% off on top of the sales price," I'd shout as I found a bargain. I'm convinced my love of numbers came from these shopping trips.

We didn't have phones those days with fancy calculators, so I'd work the math in my head, trying to find the "best" deal possible. Even the day I went to buy my first wedding dress, I marched into the store and made my way to the clearance area. I had to find a dress that was on sale, after all. While the average price of a wedding dress is $1,800 to $2,400, I'm proud to report that my first wedding dress cost a mere $397. Before you turn your nose up, this dress looks like a $1,000 dress. I have a knack for finding deals and deals on items that look like a million bucks. This skill has served me well over the years. When I got married to Jeff in my second wedding, we had an intimate backyard wedding that overlooked the bay in Long Beach, California, for only $5,000. That included alcohol, food, decorations, photography, and all the rentals . . . plus, yes, my wedding dress. Maybe I should've gone into the wedding planning business.

When I was younger, I never understood why the clothes that weren't on sale never made their way into our shopping cart. "Didn't we have enough money to buy regular-priced clothes?" I often pondered. To this day, it is almost impossible for me to buy anything that isn't on sale or found on a clearance rack. Part of the journey with my relationship with money has been to find a healthy balance between always wanting to get a good deal and buying something on sale and allowing myself to buy things I love that are the regular price. Not everything has to be on sale, I tell myself often. I am still being smart financially, even if the item is full price. I'll be honest with you: It still feels utterly painful to buy regular-priced items. Here's the thing, though: I only feel this pain when shopping for clothes and shoes, things to adorn myself in. I've never gone to a restaurant and asked if they had any leftover items in the back they could whip up for me for ½ off the menu price. I'm laughing out loud at the thought of that. So why do I feel this deep-seated need to buy clothes and shoes at a discount but feel perfectly normal when I pay for food or other full-price items? This is how insane your relationship with money is and how impactful your upbringing is.

On the other hand, my dad worked long hours and usually spent at least one weekend day working. All I knew growing up was that he worked in insurance and managed a few offices. He seemed like a "big wig" because everyone coming to our house would compliment what a great life my dad had built for us. My dad is the life of the party. He's got a big personality that just draws you in. You want to be near him. When we were young, we'd venture to downtown Houston some evenings, long before the toll roads were built, and the journey would take more than an hour just to have dinner with my dad. I just assumed this was how all dads worked. If we were lucky, he'd make it home in time to grab dinner, watch an episode of *Family Ties*, and get us off to bed. That was rare, though, but it was special when it happened. I grew up thinking that to be successful, you must work long hours and slave away to make a lot of money. Those were the rules of engagement between your career and money. The funny thing is that I don't have any conscious remorse or ill feelings for him working all those hours. I just thought this was how a dad made money for his family. It's what parents do.

From my mom, I saw a woman who would give away her last penny if she could help someone, especially her kids. Whenever I asked her for money to buy the latest Barbie accessory or head down the street to the local grab-and-go market for an orange Creamsicle, she'd dig her hands into her wallet and pull out some cash with annoying ease. She always had a smile on her face, too. There was never a begrudging tone or muddled words under her breath of discontentment. To this day, I *long* to embrace the carefree elements of my mom and her relationship with money. It seems relaxed and easy, even though I know that is far from the truth. Since we never overtly talked about money in my early years, like never, I didn't understand how to balance those two different money identities. Was I supposed to be more like my mom or my dad? Was one person's relationship with money right and the other wrong? Was it okay if I had a different relationship with money? Did I have a choice in any of this? There can be many dizzying questions about money when you are a child, even if you don't have the vocabulary to put it into words.

. . .

 MONEY TRUTH OR DARE

TRUTH: Are you getting paid what you're worth? If the answer is no, what can you do to change that?
DARE: Listen to one podcast episode today about a money topic you want to learn about.

. . .

MONEY IDENTITIES

Experts agree that your money identity is formed by the <u>age of seven</u>. Let that sink in for a minute. I don't know about you, but I can't remember much from my life before age seven. Sure, the highlights stand out, but what about the small, nuanced moments when your brain and body were trying to figure out how money worked? Those memories are hard to tap into. Between playing with your friends and doing everything to get out of completing your homework, you collected clues and beliefs about money, which became a part of your money identity, almost like your DNA. Your internal operating system.

These clues and beliefs stick with you and inform your money decisions in the background. That's the hard part. If I'm honest, you don't often know what is happening. The truth is, these money patterns are so much a part of you from an early age and are likely repeated to this day. It's like an auto-pilot mode that you run whether you like it or not. When you start to do this uncovering process, don't be surprised if you have several *aha* moments.

Here's a little experiment to work on without shame and judgment. Be brave and think about the money goals that you have that you never quite seem to reach. Or habits around money that you repeat, even though you know they aren't good for you. Then, think about your parents or whoever raised you. Can you see any similar patterns or beliefs you hold today? Can you see how your views on money might keep you from moving forward toward your goals? Conversely, do you want to embrace any good patterns or beliefs from your upbringing going forward? These patterns can work both ways.

Even in a good upbringing, your money identity can be hard to figure out. I didn't grow up having to worry about money. I never heard my parents overtly say that they were struggling financially or that we had to choose between paying the mortgage or affording clothes. Struggle wasn't a part of my money story growing up. So, you would think, how does someone like myself have a negative relationship with money? If it were that simple, I wouldn't be writing this book. No matter how you were raised, you received messages that shaped your money identity and how you interact with money today. I've made this my life's work to study and examine how what we learned from childhood shapes us as adults. This might be the first time you have made some of these connections. No matter your upbringing or when you're learning about it, you've got stuff just like the rest of us that you need to work through to get into a healthy relationship with money.

You are human; part of life is receiving mixed messages about money. If you've never done this, I dare you to try it. Pay attention to the commercials the next time you watch a TV show. Notice just how many commercials there are about something related to money. I do this experiment often, and sometimes I'm shocked that probably 70–90% of commercials are related to money. You constantly receive messages about money reinforcing fears, likely developed from childhood. Will you have enough money? Will you run out of money? What if you don't have the latest gadget, will you not be held in high regard by strangers?

I can see a direct line to both of my parents' money identities present with me. I am a risk-taker, just like my dad. I also can hyper-focus on money and believe that if I worked a bit harder, I would have more money and be happier in life, like my dad. I also always offered to treat my friends to dinner or buy a special present for their birthday, and I'd spend any sum of money to make sure my husband was happy and content, just like I saw my mom do. Sometimes, it feels like a war inside me, trying to battle and balance these two drastically different money identities. I never know which identity is winning. What I'm learning, and hopefully bringing to your world, is that we need to be aware of how we were raised regarding money, get some level of acceptance about it, and then find our own money identity that we want to carry forward.

. . .

 ## YOUR RELATIONSHIP WITH MONEY IS. . .

A conversation with Hannah Williams, CEO of Salary Transparent Street

Shannah: If you had to describe your relationship to money as a cartoon character, who would it be?

Hannah: My first thought is Squidward because it's not great, but, he's very mature. I would consider him to be the most mature 'adult' there. He's bopping about life; sometimes things are rough, sometimes he's stressed. But you're getting there and doing the best you can.

Shannah: What's one money mistake you wish you could get a do-over for?

Hannah: I have so many! An early one that comes to mind, though, is not starting to save early enough and waiting too long to start building credit. I started working at 16 at my local Pizza Hut, and I've been working ever since. In high school, I didn't save a single penny from any of my paychecks; I spent every last dime on clothes, food, and entertainment with my friends. While I wouldn't have cut those expenses out, I definitely could have cut back and started building a nest. I also waited until after college to get my first credit card because my parents were incredibly 'anti-debt' and told me they were dangerous.

While they should absolutely be used responsibly, I didn't know that they could be very helpful to start building a credit history. To this day, my credit history is still the lowest grade on my credit report because of those years I missed out on.

. . .

THE FOUR MONEY IDENTITIES

Understanding your money identity is pivotal to unlocking the hidden parts of your money story that keep you stuck. Your money identity can form a bridge to a new and healthy relationship with money because you understand how you innately interact with money. You can dive even deeper and trace your money identity lineage back generations. How does your parents' money identity differ from yours and your grandparents'? Spouse? Did they go through any social or economic events that shaped their attitudes toward money? What parts of their money identity did you pick up and carry with you today? Answering these questions is like playing a real-life game of Clue. You're piecing together the puzzle of how your money identity shapes how you show up in the world.

My friend Cedric loves digging deep into his family history. When Ancestry.com launched, he was one of the first to sign up and do his DNA profile. He knew his family immigrated to the United States in the early 1900s from South Africa and landed in Brooklyn, New York. He had heard stories from his parents about his great-grandparents and some of their struggles to move out of Africa to the States. His great-grandfather was rather wealthy in South Africa and owned a lodge in Botswana. When his grandmother was young, they moved one day out of the blue to the United States. He never really knew why and anytime he would ask, his parents and grandparents would change the conversation. Cedric had a deep desire to understand his lineage and took a trip to South Africa to meet with a genealogist. He Face-Timed me from South Africa not long after he arrived. He had learned that his ancestors were indeed very wealthy. They had property passed down from generation to generation, and his great-grandparents had amassed a fortune. They were risk-takers and created a very unique vacation spot that celebrities and dignitaries traveled all over the world to visit. However, in the late 1800s, his great-grandfather had been part of a scandal in Botswana and, as a result, lost their fortune and property. The family moved to the United States to start over and escape all the negativity they faced in South Africa. "Shannah, I can't believe what I found. So many things make sense to me now. My dad has always been so hush-hush about the family, and he's never wanted to take risks in his career or with his money. I've struggled the same way and never understood why. It's like an identity around money that we've attached ourselves to and can't shake loose," he shared. Uncovering his family history was a building block in helping Cedric understand his money identity and how he related to money. It shook him to his core, but it was a wake-up call that helped him lean into his money strengths and work through some of his weak spots.

There are four money identities, and you will largely fall into one category. Each money identity has its own strengths and weaknesses, so it's less of a game of which one is better and more of a game of, oh, now I understand myself a little better.

The Nightingale

- This person is always worried about money and decisions around money.
- This person is tense around money. Think alarm bells going off anytime someone talks about money. They often shy away from money conversations at all costs. A Nightingale might have difficulties talking about money in a relationship and need some gentle encouragement to share their thoughts and feelings without blame.
- This person tends to be conservative and risk-averse. For example, this person might want to start saving for retirement but is stuck thinking they will lose their money, so why bother? Did you see what happened to the stock market in 2009, no thank you!
- If this is you, work on building your money self-confidence and encourage yourself to take calculated risks. If you've never done

so before, take an investing risk tolerance quiz (there are tons online for free) that will determine how risky you are as an investor and offer up suggested asset allocation models to fit your level of risk. It is important to grow your money above and beyond inflation and investing is a great way to achieve that goal. Also, notice when you feel triggered the most around money. What is happening and who are you around?

Your wonderful strength is that you are a pro at saving money. You often save rather than invest and have a healthy emergency fund, just in case.

The Lion

- This person has a go big or go home mentality.
- Often, the Lion will be somewhat of a shopaholic and loves to flaunt their purchases. Status is very important to a Lion, and they like very much to stand out.
- This person is a lavish spender and often fueled by having fun above all else.
- This person can be a bit impulsive when making spending decisions. For example, your friends want to go on a vacation, and even though you've set a goal of saving for your dream home, the immediate dopamine hit of booking the trip becomes too hard to pass up.
- This person strongly needs approval and often spends money to impress others. They can become bitter when others aren't as impressed with how they are spending their money.
- This person can easily go over budget, and money matters go to the back burner. They may overlook having a budget or spending plan all together. Why bother? That would only limit their spending capabilities.
- If this is you, work on building more accountability to yourself, and create a Mindful Spending Plan (we'll cover how to do that later on) with automation built in so your money flows toward your goals without you having to choose to spend on a lavish

trip or save for retirement. From an emotional standpoint, think about where the need to impress others with your purchases comes from. Is there some other need in your life that you need to address?

Your strength is your ability to inspire others to take risks, pursue their dreams, and live life to the fullest. We all need a little Lion inside of us.

The Turtle

- The Turtle emphatically wants to take on as little debt as possible and often views having debt as a negative personal quality.
- This person tries to avoid loans, credit cards, car loans, or a mortgage.
- This person is willing to take on minimal risk and prefers simple living (the slow-and-steady approach to life). They will invest but tend to be fairly conservative in their investments.
- If this is you, work on your mindset and beliefs about taking on loans and risk. Simple living is great, but is it costing you a full and richly lived life? Also, examine your fears around debt. Where do they come from?

Your strength is that you are great at tracking your money and don't often equate fun with spending money. Turtles love a great spreadsheet.

The Wolf

- The Wolf achieves certain goals with careful risk and calculation. For example, "By 30, I want to be a millionaire, and here's what I need to do to reach that goal."
- This person has lifestyle goals they want to achieve, which are clearly defined.
- This person plans well for the future and usually has a solid investing practice of balancing risk versus return.

▪ If this is you, focus on staying within your budget and taking less risk to reach your goals. I'd also advise taking a risk tolerance quiz and determining the right asset allocation for your level of risk.

Your strength is that you have the ability to focus on your goals and what you must do to reach them. You are motivated to the core.

. . .

UNRAVELING THOUGHT #5

Think of your money identity as the operating system within which your money decisions are made. But know that you can hit shift, alt, delete, and reboot your identity at any point in life.

. . .

 TRY THIS...

Before you obsess over your money identity, I want you to do a simple assignment to help you uncover your strengths and your not-so-strengths (I really dislike the word *weaknesses*). Take out a sheet of blank paper; on one side, label it Strengths, and on the other, label it Not-So-Strengths. Let's work on the not-so-strengths side first. Write down as many struggles you can think about with money that you have. For example, I'm afraid to spend money; I love to shop when I'm emotional; my partner and I always argue about money; I overdraft my account occasionally, etc. Don't get bogged down with this side. Just try to be as objective as possible. Next to each item, write down how this hurts or prevents you from reaching your goals. Let's say one of your not-so-strengths is you are afraid to spend money. Next to that item, you might write that you don't spend money on things that will bring you joy. Now, let's move on to the good side, your strengths. Write down as many good things as you can think about in terms of how you interact with money. For example, I'm a great saver; I always find deals, I love cooking at home versus eating out, my friends always come to me for money advice, I contribute to my 401(k) every month, I can talk about money without any anxiety, etc. Go wild and list as many things as you can think of. Next to each strength, list out how that strength helps you, i.e. contributing to my 401(k) – I'm building wealth.

Once you have your list completed, go back to the not-so-strengths side. I want you to pick one item on your list and ask yourself how to turn that into a strength. If you go back to being afraid to spend money, maybe you compromise and set up a "fun" spending account where you allow yourself a certain amount of money each month to spend on things that bring you joy. In essence, you're working to create a bit of a balance between the things you're good at when it comes to money and the things you struggle with. Another great tip is to find a friend or relative with strengths where you struggle. Ask them to mentor you or help you develop more strength with money in that area. Remember, talking about money openly is a good thing. I know it can be scary, but the whole goal is to move you into a place where you stress less about money and start living more.

RELATIONSHIPS AND MONEY. . .IT'S COMPLICATED

My husband, Jeff, grew up in a completely different way than I did. His childhood was less than ideal. Jeff's parents divorced when he was eight years old, and he was given the confusing direction that he had to become the "man of the house," whatever that means to an eight-year-old. Within a year after his parent's divorce, they were both remarried, and stepparents entered the picture. Jeff's mom had primary custody of him and his siblings, and they shuffled off to his dad's house every other weekend. His parents would squabble over child support payments and put Jeff in the middle, becoming a mediator for their post-marriage difficulties. On top of that, Jeff's new stepfather was either starting or ending one of his many careers, and while they were never homeless, they had to move quite frequently to more than a dozen different homes in one city during his formative years. This is just the Cliff Notes version of his childhood and the impactful events that shaped his money story today.

Jeff picked up a fear of money, always expecting it to run out, to be difficult and elusive, and a belief that the best he could do in life was just get by. Fast-forward all these years later, he brings these beliefs from childhood that have formed his money identity into our relationship. And I bring my money identity equally to the table. He often says, "I don't know if I know how to make money. I'm unsure if anyone in my family knows how to create any kind of generational wealth." There's a direct correlation between that belief around money and the identity that he formed as a child. In case you're wondering, Jeff is a Nightingale, and as you might expect. I'm on the other end of the spectrum as a Lion.

Jeff and I were "set up" the modern-day way through Match.com. I had three solid requirements for all my Match.com dates. First, I only responded to men who first sent me a message. Second, I would only go out on a coffee date as the first date. Third, you had to offer to pay for my coffee, or else I promised myself I would leave. I'm all about financial equality when it comes to dating, but honestly, I just wanted to feel special on these dates. I had seen Jeff's profile for a few days. He caught my eye because of the line from a U2 song that he used as his profile tagline, "Stop helping God across the road like a little old lady." One Wednesday afternoon, after a long financial planning meeting, I got into my coziest pajamas and pulled a chair up to my computer. I looked at Jeff's profile one more time and sent him a message. "Hi, Game411@match.com. I like your profile song lyrics. U2 is my favorite band, so I just wanted to reach out and say hi. I've been seeing your profile for a few days now," I typed. To my surprise, I got a response just a few minutes later. "Wow, I am very impressed; that is a true U2 fan, knowing that line. That is very cool! I think even most U2 'fans' did not buy the last album. Yes, me and the boys go way back too. I can't stand the term profile, so I will say, you are very interesting. What do you do for a living with your three degrees? Jeff," he wrote.

Since I broke the first rule, I might as well break the others. We met that Friday night at Santa Monica Place, an outdoor mall near the beach. As I approached the last three escalators, I saw Jeff standing near the railing with a bright red rose. It was a cool January day in Santa Monica, and I wore my caramel-colored pea coat that I thought accentuated my bleached blonde short hair. "Hi, I'm Shannah," I said as we both went in for a hug. "I figured so. I'm Jeff. Hey, I was thinking, how about we go to this restaurant here that looks nice and sit outside," he said softly. As we walked into the restaurant and the waiter ushered us to our table, I could see Jeff sizing me up from behind. I hope he liked what he saw. We sat down in probably the most idyllic spot. Right next to a roaring outdoor fire. Under a dimly candle-lit table. We chit-chatted for a few minutes, trying to eliminate the collective nerves when the waiter came to our table. "What can I get you both to drink," he said. I instantly had the most aggressive money talk in my head. Do I order a vodka on the rocks like I want to, knowing it is expensive?

Am I assuming, or even expecting, that he pays for dinner? Should I let him order a drink first and gauge my order on his? Why am I actually expecting my date to pay for me? Isn't that old-school logic? What if I do want him to pay for me? Does that make me a shallow person? My mom always says men should pay for the meal; it's tacky if the woman pays or is expected to pay. More importantly, which money identity was he, and would he complement mine, as this was the second time around finding love?

Relationships and money are tricky. You've got two different people with different money stories and identities. Things can clash, especially if you haven't done the work to understand your money identity and how you interact with money. I encourage you to deeply understand your money identity and lovingly share it with your partner. I wish these money conversations and discoveries were required to get into a relationship, and certainly marriage. I think it would help lower the divorce rate substantially. At least, that's my hope.

QUESTIONS TO PONDER

1. What money personality do you relate the most to?
2. What are your money strengths and weaknesses?
3. What's one thing you want to learn about money in the next 30 days?
4. Can you see patterns in your money personality to either of your parents?

CHAPTER 6

What's Your Money Pie?

t was a blistering hot 105-degree Saturday morning in early July when I met my friend Cassandra for coffee at our favorite local hangout spot. Per usual, I was there 15 minutes early to snag my favorite table by the window when I saw Cassandra nervously enter the cafe. I could tell she was flustered by how she shifted her purse in her arms. Her eyes danced around the coffee shop, looking for me, even though I knew she saw me in the window as she walked up.

She came to the table, threw her purse down, scrounged around for her phone, and said, "I need your help. I'm thinking of quitting my job, and all of a sudden, I've been overwhelmed with terrible feelings about my worth and money, and honestly, I just feel like shit." I paused to wait for her to finish. "I can't. I can't figure money out. I'm 44 years old in a few days, I don't have any retirement, I need to find something new, I'm scared, and I don't know why, and I can never ever reach any of the money goals I want to. I feel embarrassed and ashamed of myself, and I have never shared that out loud with anyone. There's something wrong with me, right?" Cassandra shouted with tears streaming down her face.

That's a lot to dump out on a Saturday morning when I had already broken a full-on sweat just walking from my car to the coffee shop a few feet away. I wiped the beads of sweat off my forehead and asked Cassandra to grab five napkins and a pen. I needed to show her something I had been working on called the Money Pie approach. She wasn't too happy that we were going to talk about money before we loaded our plates with food, but I encouraged her to hear this. I wanted Cassandra, for the first time, to have a long look at the negative money thoughts and self-talk that were playing on repeat in her head. Like most money stories in our heads, these thoughts are not productive and helpful. With my instruction, Cassandra perked up, leaped over the counter, and grabbed the napkins. I could tell she was ready to dump these thoughts about money that had plagued her for so very long. As a money expert, it's always interesting for me to witness when someone hits their breaking point with money and desperately wants to make changes.

THE MONEY PIE APPROACH

The Money Pie is something that I created after working for more than 10 years with clients, sitting elbow to elbow with them as we created a plan for their financial future. Fresh off the press, I would watch clients metaphorically throw their financial plans in the trash and continue along with how they were operating with their money. So they stayed stuck. Nothing changed. They never got any closer to reaching their money goals. They stayed anxious, frustrated, and ashamed of money. I was beginning to think that I wasn't a great financial planner until I heard the same outcomes from all my other financial planner friends. Why was this happening? It didn't make sense for people to pay good sums of money for a financial plan and direction and then not take any action. Many clients would call me back in a few months, asking for another session or an update on their financial plan. I searched for answers from my money story and beliefs, trying to unravel why I stayed stuck, unwilling to make any changes, even though I wanted to change. I knew there had to be something internally happening that a financial plan couldn't solve. So, I came up with the Money Pie approach.

. . .

 YOUR RELATIONSHIP WITH MONEY IS. . .

A conversation with Joe Saul-Sehy, host of the *Stacking Benjamins* podcast and author of *Stacked: Your Super Serious Guide to Modern Money Management*

Shannah: What's one money mistake you wish you could get a do-over for?

Joe: I've struggled with this question because I've made so many money mistakes. My fundamental money mistake was not taking the concept of "OPM" seriously. Finance shortcut people online always tell you to "use other people's money" to get ahead. I landed in tons of credit card debt because I borrowed so much money and never had a plan to repay it. I was just going to magically buy stuff that would help me make more money, and that would then translate to riches. I think this is the "big lie" in society. "If I just make more money, my problems will go away." I'm here to say that they do not. It doesn't matter how much money you make; bad habits will bury you. I had first to lock down my budget and THEN make more money to widen the gap between what I made and what I brought home.

Shannah: What's one money splurge you'd never give up?

Joe: Anyone who knows me knows I have a slight addiction to board games. When I get a group of friends together and dive into a game, we're all having so much fun laughing about what each other is doing. We often get off on these tangents about just each other's lives, and truly, for me, it is a way to get more connection and get lost in it in a very playful way, so I don't think I'll ever give it up. Everybody who knows me will tell you I don't need to buy another one, but I will keep buying them. I like a game called Viticulture, where you own a winery. It's super-fun setting up your winery, shipping orders for people, and building your winery to win.

· · ·

The Money Pie borrows from an approach from Cognitive Behavioral Therapy (CBT) called The Cognitive Triangle. The Cognitive Behaviorial Therapy triangle is a method therapists use to teach the process of changing negative thought patterns. It works like this – your thoughts influence your feelings, and your feelings influence your actions. If you can change your thoughts, you can change a whole chain of events. The Money Pie approach I have adapted takes this process further. It looks at your thoughts, feelings, and actions and then adds a look at your patterns and behaviors, which are important steps in cementing a whole new approach to healthily interacting with money going forward.

Humans are taught to think everything will change if we just take new actions around money. New actions include signing up for a Roth IRA, saving money, paying off credit card debt, getting a better-paying job, etc. These all seem like logical next steps. You search for actions to take, consume every book you can get your hands on, listen to all the podcasts, dissect all the blogs, and play endlessly with all the calculators that tell you if you just save this amount, life will be good. You want to know the five best ways to invest, the top tips to save money, how to earn more in your career, and so much more. You want the quick fix. But you already know this endless loop of tips doesn't solve your money worries. If it did, you wouldn't be reading this book. The Money Pie approach asks you to rethink your actions and look at them through a lens of greater understanding of your thoughts and feelings and the role your money story plays in your day-to-day money choices. The point is to have a greater awareness, *aha* discoveries, about why you make certain choices with your money.

. . .

 MONEY TRUTH OR DARE

TRUTH: Are you more resourceful or more wasteful with money?
DARE: Increase your retirement contribution by 0.5% or 1% (if you can).

. . .

MONEY, AND YOUR THOUGHTS

Let's discuss some of the most common money thoughts and beliefs and see if any of these resonate with you. If you find yourself saying *yes, that's me*, to any of the below items, please remember that these thoughts don't mean you are bad with money. If we polled a crowd of 100 people, I can guarantee many would share these thoughts and beliefs. Side note – I think that would be rather refreshing. Walking around and sharing your thoughts and beliefs about money could be refreshing. If someone could say, "Me, too. I'm so happy I'm not alone," imagine the walls we could tear down that money builds up. On to the list:

- It's too late for me to learn about money
- I make good money but don't have anything to show for it
- I'm no good with money and shouldn't be trusted with it
- I always waste money
- I've made too many money mistakes, and I'm just going to keep making them

- My partner is always mad at me because I save my money wisely and don't spend
- I'm a disappointment to my parents because I'm not as wealthy as I should be
- I always settle for less than my worth in my job, and I guess that's how it will always be
- I never make good choices with my money
- I'm always going to be living paycheck-to-paycheck; I should just get used to it
- If I made more money, I'd be a lot happier in life
- I'm always going to be stressed out about money. . .isn't everyone?

Let me offer you some relief here. These are very common money thoughts and beliefs that almost *every* human has. When you have one of these thoughts, it becomes embedded into your core belief system and greatly impacts the choices you make or don't make with your money. Let's take "It's too late for me to learn about money" as an example. If this is your core thought and belief, the feelings it might evoke are shame, guilt, fear, frustration, and more. Any of those feelings are not great motivators for taking intentional and mindful action with your money. Instead, you might choose never to look at your bank account, may never want to talk about money, or just flat-out quit trying to learn more about the parts of money that seem daunting.

What normally happens is you look for confirmations in the world that affirm your thought that it's too late for you to learn about money. If you have a surprise bill come up, or you forget to pay something, or let's say you get your tax refund and then go to move it to your savings account only to find that money is missing (ahem, spent) from your bank account, all of those situations reaffirm your thought that it's too late for you to learn about money so you're just going to quit. You are looking for tiny moments in your day-to-day life that say things to you like, "Yes, see, there, it's too late for you. You will keep making these decisions with money that don't help you. Look at you. You're never going to learn how to (invest, save, spend wisely)." Reading this, it's easy to see how you essentially self-destruct when it comes to money. Internally, you can say the worst things to yourself, and you believe those thoughts. The problem is that your brain and body can't separate what is fact from fiction. That's where the work comes in.

For the longest time, I had a goal of making my podcast financially viable. I started my podcast, originally called *Millennial Money*, in 2015 before podcasts were a thing. I still remember a day early on when my phone blew up with messages. My little podcast was #2 on the Top of the Charts, above Rachel Maddow and other top shows. I could never understand how that happened. It was crazy to me that people were tuning in to hear me talk about money. When my podcast started to gain sponsors, I was so thrilled. I began to think that earning a living with a podcast was possible. The problem is I was stuck in some old money thought patterns that did not help me. On one hand, I was still not certain I could make it as an entrepreneur and always had the belief in the back of my head that I would have to give up this pursuit and just go get a "regular" job. On the other hand, when I did start making very good money from the podcast, I froze, disbelieving it could carry on. No matter the situation, I was trapped in the negative thought patterns that kept me from thriving financially. This is a very common occurrence for entrepreneurs like myself. You start to get a taste of financial success and then you freak yourself out and bring your income level back down.

. . .

UNRAVELING THOUGHT #6

Years of bad money thoughts require some sort of inertia to create change. This process won't happen overnight, but if you string together enough supportive and healthy money thoughts, you'll be surprised at how fast you feel like a completely different person. Give it a try.

. . .

The Money Pie approach works like this:

Thoughts Influence Feelings.

Feelings Influence Actions.

Actions Influence Patterns.

Patterns Influence Behaviors.

You must start by changing your money inputs to change your money outcomes.

Your first step is choosing good **thoughts** about money and your goals. For example, instead of, "I'm never good with money, no one in my family ever was, and nothing is ever going to change that," swap your thought for something like, "I have the power to create the financial future I want for myself apart from my family, and it starts today."

Legendary comedian Paula Poundstone was a guest on the *Everyone's Talkin' Money* podcast, and she decided she would break up with money after being one million dollars in debt. That's a capital M and six zeros! She said, "My kids would come to me and ask if we could go to Disneyland, and I'd say, well, I don't see why not. It took me years to work on my negative thinking about money, and honestly, it's still a work in progress. I would say that's true for most of us." Creating a better thought is hard when you're in a tough financial position. That I know very personally to be true. I advise you that a better thought that feels good doesn't cost anything, so why not try it on and see how it fits? Every . . . single . . . time . . . I do this process, I feel better. I feel more encouraged. My money situation hasn't changed, but I've changed.

Negative money thoughts create a cyclic nature that is hard to escape. Here's how this cycle works:

1. Negative money thoughts impact your mental health. You feel pretty bad about yourself.
2. When you have these negative feelings, managing your money is harder. You want to avoid it at all costs. You might be looking for a quick fix to solve your money issues.
3. This leads to more money problems. And the cycle continues.

If you want to get off the thought rollercoaster, I have a great exercise. I call it Money Bubbles. Whenever one of those pesky negative thoughts about money comes into your mind, visualize placing that thought into a bubble and pushing it out of your mind. It's like swiping right every time a negative or unproductive thought about money comes up and moving on to a better thought. It takes some practice, but it gets easier and easier the more money bubbles you push away.

Your thoughts then influence your **feelings**. If your new thought is, "I have the power to create the financial future I want for myself apart from my family, and it starts today," what kind of feeling does that new thought evoke? Maybe something like, "I feel excited when I look at my money." Now you're getting somewhere.

The Feelings Wheel, or Wheel of Emotions, is a helpful tool to discover your emotions and feelings. There are six core emotions: joy, love, fear, anger, sadness, and surprise. Within each core emotion are secondary emotions such as grief, frustration, nervousness, optimism, and so on. And within those secondary emotions is another outer band of emotions. In Brené Brown's brilliant book, *Atlas of the Heart*, she details 87 emotions and experiences that define what it means to be a human. She surveyed more than 7,000 people for five years and found that those surveyed could only identify three emotions: happiness, sadness, and anger.

One of my biggest life lessons has been understanding my feelings in circumstances. I have always been a people pleaser and tend to take on the feelings and emotions of others around me. I know it's not healthy, but it's what I know. Whenever my therapist asks me how I feel when we start a session, I'm banned from quipping back, "I'm good." In her words, "Good is not a feeling." If you've never looked at the Feelings Wheel, I suggest you do. Who knew there were that many emotions and feelings that we could feel?

Your feelings then become the motivators for the **actions** you take. Instead of choosing an action that affirms your negative thoughts and feelings, you can now choose actions that affirm your positive and motivating thoughts and feelings. "I'm so motivated to take action because I feel excited. I will look at my bank account balance, remove any subscriptions I don't need, and then put that savings into my credit card balance I'm working on paying off." You're starting to make progress.

The more action you take, the more healthy **patterns** emerge, and those patterns become healthy **behaviors**. Something seemingly simple, like you want to save a certain amount of money but have never been able to use The Money Pie approach, can help you unravel your feelings and move forward with a new perspective. You understand why you want to save money, and it then gives you feel-good vibes; you are motivated to set up an auto-debit from your bank account each month so the money flows without you thinking, and that creates a pattern and ultimately a behavior that saving money is non-negotiable. These new patterns and behaviors help you reach your money goals with greater ease. It's not to say that bumps along the road won't come up or that you won't have to work hard at this process, but it gives you a framework and a direction to follow that does create inner and outer changes with your money.

 ## TRY THIS...

Since this is all a new way of thinking about money, let's back into the process of creating a new thought slowly and gently. This process might feel a little clunky in the beginning. Remember, your brain is lazy and wants to keep following the same patterns around money you have for years. Starting to think new thoughts is like jumpstarting a car that has stalled out. You're working on a new muscle, so to speak, so be patient with yourself in this process.

Let's start with your current money situation.

Step 1:

What truth or circumstance is present right now with your money?

Instead of saying, "I have a lot of debt," write down $5K in credit card debt. Instead of saying, "I'm bad at money," write down, "I spent $500 last weekend." Try to be very specific about the current truth or circumstance in your life.

Truth or Circumstance _____

What is a thought around that truth or circumstance that bubbles up to the surface? For example, "I am always living paycheck-to-paycheck or I don't have anything to show for the money I've made."

Thought_____

How do you feel when you believe this thought? (Be honest.)

Feelings _____

What action steps do you take when you feel this way? (*None* is an acceptable answer.)

Actions_____

What is the result or the outcome of these actions?

Outcome_____ (Stuck, Frustrated, etc.)

Can you see how these thoughts create a negative cascade? Who is motivated to stress less about money or make better money decisions when you're telling yourself that you are terrible with money? Or, maybe you're stuck thinking you grew up with a terrible financial upbringing and there's no way you'll have enough money. Or, maybe you grew up in a healthy family environment, but you're stuck trying to make progress toward your goals. Who can blame you with destructive money thoughts roaming your head all day? Money and life are stressful enough. I'm a big fan of finding a kinder, less worry-filled way to interact with money. What do you think?

Step 2:

So let's change things starting now. How about we look at intentional thoughts and how they change your outcome? You'll choose a new, kind, gentler, supportive thought about money. I find starting with your desired outcome or result easier and working around that.

Imagine what you would *like* to have in your life. Be very specific and create a separate thought line for each result. You can use this process over and over again. Remember, we are re-training how you think, act, and feel about money. Use the same truth or circumstance as above, such as "I have $5,000 of credit card debt."

Current Truth or Circumstance_____

What outcome would you like to achieve instead? For example, "I'd like to have $0 credit card debt."

Outcome_____

What action steps would you take to reach this outcome? For example, "I need to create my spending plan, remove my credit card from online shopping carts, and meal plan each week." What do you need to do for that outcome to be achieved?

Actions_____

How would you need to feel to be able to take these action steps? For example, motivated, excited, encouraged, hopeful, etc.

Feelings_____

What is a super-small, believable thought you could have to feel this way? For example, "I can pay off my credit card debt or I do make good choices with my money."

Thought_____

See how much better that feels? A circumstance that you thought was not doable just a minute ago became a circumstance with a bit more hope. I encourage you to walk through this process for all your current money truths and circumstances. Let these new money thoughts serve as motivation to create momentum that pushes you toward your goals and not away from them.

THE MONEY PIE APPROACH IN ACTION

Cassandra returned to the table and threw the five napkins before me. "If you can help me figure this out, I owe you every penny to my name," she said softly. "Let's start with napkin #1 and label it Thoughts," I instructed.

Thoughts – Cassandra's overwhelming thoughts around money were that no matter what she did, she would never make good money choices. She would always be "behind the curve," so to speak. I let Cassandra select what her new thoughts about money would be. "Each day, I choose healthy thoughts around money that will have a positive ripple effect. I'm choosing to say to myself, it's not too late to reach my money goals, and today I'm making progress." I like how this sounds. Her face lit up. . .with a healthy degree of skepticism of the process.

Feelings – Cassandra felt her chest tighten up and an intense sense of anxiety whenever she thought about money. "It sometimes feels like a volcano is about to erupt inside me. I can't feel anything but shame and fear repeatedly," Cassandra told me. Instead, we focused on a box breathing technique to help release Cassandra's anxiety in those volcano moments. The box breathing technique works like this: four breaths in, hold for four counts, breathe out for four counts, and hold again for four counts. Once she went through a round or two of box breathing, I asked her to check in with her feelings about her new positive thoughts about money. "I'm starting to believe that I do make good money choices each day. I feel more motivated to tackle things on my money to-do list that have lingered for a while now. These things would've terrorized me in the past," she said a few weeks after our coffee date.

Actions – Cassandra wasn't sure what action steps to take to start building up a retirement account. She'd get lost in her overwhelming thoughts about how far behind she was from everyone else and how she would never be able to retire. On her napkin, we charted out a few small steps she could take this month to affirm her new thought: (i) open up a Roth IRA account, (ii) take $100 extra that she had and deposit it into the account, (iii) choose an index fund or target date fund with a low expense ratio to invest in, (iv) reward herself for taking these steps. When I checked with her a few weeks later, she told me how encouraging it felt to do something with her money. "Shannah, I swear, I doubted this whole Money Pie process, but honestly, I laugh at myself often. These little new thoughts about money started to help me feel better. Even my friends are noticing that I have a smile on my face more often. I tell them it's the Money Pie's fault and leave them wondering what I'm talking about."

Patterns – New patterns are important when it comes to money. Patterns turn into habits, good habits. You start repeating a set of actions without thinking. How second nature is it to brush your teeth before you go to bed? You do this repeatedly because you've told yourself that brushing your teeth is a smart action each night. Your teeth thank you, and so does your partner. With Cassandra, we set up some healthy patterns around money that would be easy for her to accomplish.

- The box breathing exercise when she felt a sense of money anxiety
- A 24-hour spending pause where she could put items in her cart online but had to wait 24 hours to purchase to decide if she needed or wanted the item
- A weekly Money Date where she checked in on her spending over the last week and looked over her goals to notice progress and make any changes
- She created an intention each morning – a healthy thought about money that she would carry with her all day long
- And, practically speaking, Cassandra set up an auto-debit of $100 monthly into her new Roth IRA and picked a few funds to invest in

Behaviors – Behaviors take time, especially when we're dealing with money changes. However, taking some small steps and setting up a space for healthy thoughts and feelings around money tricks your brain into believing anything really is possible. For Cassandra, it took about 60 days until she was running on autopilot and continuing to build on all the positive steps in the Money Pie. Her new way of thinking became the biggest behavioral change.

I want to be really honest with you and say that creating new thoughts and feelings about money is super-hard work. It is like pushing a boulder up a hill most days. I've had the idea to write this book for a while now, and you better believe the minute I sat down to write page one, all of my money fears, worries, and negative thoughts bubbled to the surface. I've realized that my pretty terrible messy relationship with money continues because of the thoughts that I allow in my head. Despite my best efforts, I tend to have a million negative thoughts before I can muster up the courage to have a good thought. I don't know how your experience is related to money thoughts, but I sure hope I'm not alone in this cycle of thinking. I have difficulty refraining from beating myself up for past money decisions I've made. On days when my thoughts are in the gutter, I do whatever I can to dislodge my brain from its malicious thought patterns. On some days, I operate on a minute-by-minute basis, doing wherever I can to create some distance between my first horrible thought and my second horrible thought.

The solace that I feel is knowing that negative thinking around money affects so many of us. I've had the opportunity to talk to people worldwide and ask them deep and intruding questions about their relationship with money. Most people fidget a bit before answering, "Tell me what money thoughts are running on repeat in your head today." It's challenging to vocalize these thoughts because they aren't very nice for most of us, and that's putting it mildly. The thought of millions of people on this Earth operating every day with hurtful internal monologues brings me a great deal of sadness. I'm not a philosopher, but why do we all let this happen? Maybe the answer isn't in wanting to undo our entire financial system. Maybe the answer is learning to turn off the TV when a commercial stresses you out – like the onslaught of commercials on 2 January of every year about tax time.

There's nothing like a tax commercial to end a good New Year's Day hangover. Maybe the answer is deciding not to read that online article about stocks having their worst day and how your portfolio is doomed. Maybe the answer is getting more in touch with who you are and who you want to be and letting go of who people want you to be. I call this values-based money. Acknowledging your money story and devising a money plan that works toward your values, rather than getting sucked up in the money messages of others that don't serve you.

Whatever the answer, I know the starting place is with you and your inner thoughts. I'm going to create a bumper sticker as a reminder that if you want to make outside changes with your money, you first need to do the inside work.

QUESTIONS TO PONDER

1. Would you classify yourself as a spender or saver, and why?
2. What is your go-to thing to splurge on, and why?
3. If someone dropped $10,000 into your bank account without strings attached, how would you use it and why? (The answer to this question gives clues to the action steps you should take with your money right now).
4. Write down your money thoughts for one day. Put a plus sign next to your positive thoughts and a negative sign next to your negative thoughts. Look back at the end of the day and take stock of what thoughts were motivators for you during the day. For example, when your partner didn't compliment you this morning, did you react by buying something that made you feel better, stopping for coffee when you didn't need it, etc.? What I love about this question is that it asks you to discover your thoughts from a curiosity perspective, not a judgmental one.

CHAPTER **7**

What Are Your
Money Patterns?

ou never know when your life will change in a second. Mine did. You never know what would happen if you lost one of your senses and you'd never be able to hear the world in the same way again. That's my life now.

I grabbed a cup of my favorite Chamomile Lemon tea, and headed to my usual morning yoga class with Jeff, about ten minutes from our house. We arrived in the waiting area as we had so many days that year with our yoga mats and water bottles in hand. The waiting area was always quiet, so we whispered about the day and where we wanted to eat lunch afterward. I wanted to go to Islands, a tropical-themed restaurant with tasty burgers and fries. Burgers and fries were always my go-to meal whenever I was asked to choose a restaurant. After our five-minute discussion about which burger we would each have, I felt an uncomfortable heaviness in my left ear and an eerie sudden silence. It felt like someone had turned off the light switch on my left ear, and all the sounds were missing. Gone. Vanished.

I grabbed Jeff's arm with panic, "I think something is wrong. For some reason, I can't hear out of my left ear. And there's a loud buzzing noise that's happening internally." "What do you mean all of a sudden," he whispered. "I don't know. Something just happened. It feels very strange," I could barely get the words out. It's got to be ear wax or something strange, for sure, I thought. What else could it be?

We took our usual spots in the back of the yoga class and rolled out our mats. I couldn't get over the incredible buzzing sound in my ear. My brain searched through its database of possible problems, anything I could think of. Sinus infection? I never had this reaction before, if it was. Headache or migraine? I'm sure you don't lose all your hearing in one ear with a headache. Did something happen to me during my sleep? I surely would've noticed if something did; I have always been a terribly light sleeper, waking up so easily. Jeff was positioned to my left in class, and I struggled to make out the words as he tried to talk to me. "What? I can't hear you," I said repeatedly with an annoying cadence. Knowing what I know now, I should've gotten up from class and left immediately. I was not okay. For future reference, as a public service announcement, if you ever find yourself in this situation, head straight to the emergency room and get a dose of steroids. That's the best option to try to recover your hearing.

I fumbled through the yoga class, straining at best to hear the teacher's prompts. My heart was racing as I moved through the poses, scared out of my mind thinking about how uncomfortable my ear felt. After class, we made a beeline for the car, went home immediately, forgot about burgers, showered, and I felt a sinking feeling inside. Have you ever had one of those moments when you knew life would be different, and there wasn't anything you could do about it? The pressure in my ear felt like someone had dropped about ten bricks on my left side, and they were progressively pushing down on them all at once. This was a pain I had never experienced before. Take a normal headache and dial it up about a thousand times, which might come close to what it felt like. Or your worst hangover compounded by a thousand children screaming all at once in loud voices.

Weeks of doctor's appointments and audiologist tests confirmed that I now had profound deafness in my left ear. I was diagnosed with sensorineural hearing loss, better known as single-sided deafness. I had normal hearing in my right ear but a complete loss of sound and voice recognition in my left ear. Along with the deafness came 24/7 tinnitus in my left ear. Picture loud TV static at full blast constantly without stopping playing internally. It's been seven years of this unwanted visitor haunting me day and night. What a strange thing to be unable to hear anything outwardly through my left ear, but it has a lot to say internally.

What's the saying? Something good always comes from something bad. During these first few days, weeks, and months of single-sided deafness, I had an awakening of sorts. If this was my new reality, I knew I had to change how I moved through the world.

I think I've been a nervous or anxious person, probably since I was born. I remember one summer trip in the sixth grade that my family took to the East Coast. We flew into New York City, rented a car, and drove up to New Hampshire in a whirlwind few days. We got off the highway to eat at some random roadside restaurant in the middle of New Jersey, and when we went to get back on the highway, it was closed, to our surprise. A big torrential rain storm went through New Jersey earlier that day, and a giant 20-foot tree had fallen across the road, blocking all the lanes. This was long before cell phones and Google Maps to navigate our detour. It was the old-school days of paper maps, Thomas Guide style, and trying to piece together directions to get us to our destination. We must've driven around the same few New Jersey towns all day because we never made any progress toward our actual destination. I remember that experience making me so frightfully nervous that I had to stop to pee at least five times in a few hours. I'm not sure what I was so relentlessly anxious about. The idea of being lost felt overwhelming to me as a 12-year-old. This was the same nervous and anxious feeling that I felt those first few months with single-sided deafness, but I couldn't get away from it this time. It was now a part of who I am.

Doctor after doctor stressed the importance of having less stress, ideally no stress, in my life to lessen the impact of straining to hear and an overworked brain dealing with tinnitus. (Chronic tinnitus, like I have, doesn't turn off when I sleep. My brain doesn't reboot like yours does when you rest and recover. My brain is always working. So, I operate constantly in tiredness and nervous system aggravation. And yes, I produce a successful podcast with only one good ear.) Okay, how do you stress less? I started to look at the areas of my life that had been stressful, and there were quite a few areas that needed some serious TLC. Front and center was my relationship with money and the naughty money patterns, beliefs, and thoughts I had excused and left unchecked for far too long.

Losing my hearing was a not-so-gentle invitation to do life differently. I chronicled my story on a podcast episode in 2018 but haven't spoken about it publicly very often. Invisible disabilities are hard for people to understand. If you look at me, you can't tell I have hearing loss except for a few clues. I've gotten exceptionally good at straining my neck to hear you when you talk, and if we're walking together, I do a little dance around you so my good ear is always facing you. I can't locate where sound is coming from anymore. It's a very strange thing to describe. You need two good ears to locate sound; otherwise, you're constantly wondering who is talking and where a sound is coming from. Those are a few of the external factors of hearing loss. Internally, that's a whole different story. Music, which I love, doesn't sound the same, and I forget about attending loud concerts. I find it hard to be in some social situations and worry that I'm missing out on the conversation. I also worry about my future healthcare needs and the associated costs. However, hearing loss has given a lot in return. A chance to rediscover who I am as a person. I want to let go of my constant workaholic tendencies. I want to create new patterns that are healthy moving forward. Most importantly, I want to release any money worries and blocks that I feel are holding me back.

. . .

 MONEY TRUTH OR DARE

TRUTH: What is your biggest money goal?
DARE: Track your spending this week and look for any opportunities to spend more intentionally.

. . .

MONEY SECRETS

What are your biggest money secrets? We all have naughty money patterns that aren't serving us. Whether you've racked up a bunch of credit card debt (like me), made a not-so-great investment (hello crypto), spent too much on a vacation (who could blame you?), you're afraid to spend money (yes, it's a thing), or your eating-out budget is through the roof (you gotta eat, right?), your money patterns are not a sign of weakness or failure. They are just patterns that feel really comfy to you. Since money is such a taboo topic, these sneaky money patterns require forcible effort to eliminate them.

Spending money when you are down, anxious, or stressed out is how most people operate. The pattern of spending money is a dopamine hit that is very addictive. You buy stuff to fill that hole inside of you. To make you feel successful. To stand out. To feel nourished.

It just feels good. I work in reverse. I spent very little money when I was stressed out, but when I had a good month in my business, my brain would quickly think about everything I needed to spend money on. I get a bit irrational. There were always so many better choices to make with my money like investing or donating to a charity I support. Instead, another trip or shopping spree always sounded good in those moments. Staring down a heap of credit card debt, I knew I had to bring all the money tools I had taught other people front and center into my relationship with money. This is always easier said than done. Your brain is lazy, remember. It likes to stay comfortable even if it's a habit that needs to be broken.

. . .

 ## YOUR RELATIONSHIP WITH MONEY IS...

...with Anna Papalia, CEO of Interviewology and author of the book *Interviewology: The New Science of Interviewing*

Shannah: Is there a central money theme or loop that plays on repeat for you?

Anna: I do a lot of internal work on retraining my brain. Maybe it's because I'm a coach, maybe because I have done this for so long, that I'm always thinking about examining my thoughts and how to recast and reframe when I'm in a place of feeling like I'm lacking. What triggers me? How do I act afterwards? How can I do better next time? That's generally my loop that I go through. So if I feel triggered, like I go out to a nice dinner, for example, there will always be the poor little girl inside me who's like I can't believe you just spent $60 on sushi by yourself. Who do you think you are? Why did you do this? That's dumb. You could have just eaten cereal at home. That is a very common loop, I think, when it comes to people who grew up with nothing, or for me, I feel very responsible to not mess this up. So that's the loop of beating myself up that I go to, and it becomes problematic and harmful when I'm supposed to be enjoying things, and I'm still like I'll enjoy some of this success. I have a hard time just relaxing and enjoying something because I'm always thinking about well, I can't really relax too much, or I can't enjoy this too much, or you don't want to get too comfortable. That I attribute to well, I'm very ambitious and I'm never satisfied. But I've unpacked lately that that also could make me crazy and I might have a heart attack in two years. So there's that side of it.

Shannah: What is a guilty money splurge that you're never giving up?

Anna: I don't think I could ever say I'd never give anything up. I love the freedom of having options. I would say the one thing that I do every single day is I do have a nice cup of coffee every single day, Doesn't matter how poor I've been or how wealthy I am. I also own a beautiful beach house, which is my happy place, and I feel incredibly lucky to have gone from basically a homeless 15-year-old to having this incredible place that brings me so much joy, and to be so lucky that I have found a physical space that brings me joy. I don't know if I would ever say I would never give it up, but those are some things that make me so incredibly happy and satisfied.

. . .

UNRAVELING THOUGHT #7

If you're a creature of habit like me, you know how hard it is to change a pattern. The next time you find yourself in one of those patterns you'd like to break, ask yourself, "Is this pattern helping me move closer to my money goals?" If the answer is no, ask this follow-up question: "What would it look like if I did _____ differently?"

. . .

I decided it would be helpful to know some of the most common money secrets we share. I asked my podcast listeners if they would be brave enough to share some of their money secrets, secrets that they've held tucked inside, with me for the greater good of us all. I was surprised how many people were willing to share their innermost secrets openly. One listener replied, "Wow, it feels good to get these secrets off my chest and share them with you." So, I wanted to share some of the juicy secrets with you, leaving everyone anonymous.

#1 – "I have a really bad money pattern, and I guess it's a secret I've never shared with anyone. After my partner and I argue, it can be about anything, I find an immense amount of joy in shopping online for sportswear. I probably own about fifty pairs of leggings from all the different stores I've bought over the years after arguments. Here's what I'm thinking in the process: sportswear is all about getting in shape. So, I think, unrealistically, of course, if I spend money on leggings and sports bras, my partner will be so enamored by my muscular physique that they won't get mad at me about whatever topic we're arguing about. But here's where it backfires. I spend SO much on sportswear that I'm not contributing what I need for retirement, and my partner can't understand why my priorities aren't more aligned with my goals. This pattern, though, feels so good that it's hard to break." (Anonymous listener)

#2 – "Oh, money secrets. I have a lot of those. I would say my biggest money secret is that I'm afraid to invest aggressively. I have this pattern of reading all the bad articles about investing, and there are a lot of them, and then I convince myself that it's a good thing that I don't have more money invested. All of my friends always talk about having all their money in index funds. We're in our 30s, so that's totally normal. I just nod and play along. I'm embarrassed to admit that I'm totally scared of losing money. I really want to stop reading all those clickbait articles, but since I've told myself that investing is risky, they constantly reinforce that thinking. Yikes, I need an intervention." (Anonymous listener)

#3 – "I don't share bank accounts with my partner because I don't want her to see how much I spend on sports betting. I really got into it a few years ago when I lost my job and I was looking for some entertainment and a way to make a little extra cash. Every time I get a bonus check, I spend a fair amount of it on sports betting. I do pretty well, but I've lost a lot too. I can't shake this urge to bet on the teams I love. I've gone to therapy and worked through a lot of my feelings, and now I make sure to set aside a certain amount that I allow myself to bet with." (Anonymous listener)

#4 – "I micro-manage spending in my household to a fault. I lost my job about ten years ago, and now have a really good job, but I am always in fear of money running out. Plus, I like to spend money on things that matter to me but not so much on stuff that my husband enjoys, like sporting events and concerts. Every weekend he wants to go to another concert, and it's super-expensive. I get grumpy and am in a bad mood, I know. I really want to tell myself that it's okay to spend money because it is, but I keep going back to this, thinking of never having enough. Just last week I went to eat with my friends for their 40th birthday and it was really expensive. My husband asked why I'm not in a bad mood when I spend money on myself or my friends. I didn't really have an answer, and I for sure didn't tell him just how much it really cost me. Is there any hope for me?" (Anonymous listener)

#5 – "I don't know if this is really a money secret, but I spend a lot of money on vacations each year. Probably more than most people would. I like nice things. I'm always dreaming up new vacation destinations and plotting where I want to go next. I work remotely, so it makes it possible. I guess the secret is that spending money on all this travel doesn't leave me money left to save or invest. I'm 45 right now, and that feels a bit scary, but it's not enough for me to give up my trips. When my dad asks how my investments are doing, I always tell him, great, no issues here. I don't feel like I can be honest with him or anyone because I know they would judge me."

#6 – "Sometimes I have emotional days, and the only thing that will fix it is to buy something. I still like to shop in person and I'll just wander around the mall until I find something to buy. All the while inside, I'm thinking bad thoughts because there are a million things I could do with my time other than shop. I started to volunteer with an organization in town, thinking that it would help me kick the urge to shop, but it hasn't. I don't shop every day. But when work and home life are really stressful, I need that release. I know it's a bad money pattern. I figure it's better than some other vices I could pick up." (Anonymous listener)

#7 – "I secretly send money to my dad when he needs it without telling my mom or my wife. I get that this is a bad pattern, for sure. I just feel bad because my dad had a hard life, and he tried really hard to be financially independent, but the truth is he needs help. My wife can't understand why we need to send our money to my dad. My dad and mom divorced when I was young, so my mom has little sympathy for him. At first, it felt like a little secret I could carry, but the longer this goes on, the more guilt I feel for not sharing it with them. I'm not sacrificing any of our money goals so I feel comfortable with it. Mainly, I just feel responsible for my dad because he helped me out when I was younger and in college." (Anonymous listener)

Those are just seven examples of the many money secrets people shared with me. We all seem to have a little money secret hidden away that we'd rather not share if we didn't have to. As you've seen in some of these examples, money secrets often turn into good and not-so-good money patterns. One question that listeners asked me over and over again was how to break these money patterns and start to create new ones. Here are some favorite tips and techniques that I've used in my relationship with money and shared with clients over the years.

The 24-hour spending rule: I have a habit of online window shopping. I'll open a bunch of browsers and shop my favorite sites. I put everything in my shopping cart to pretend I would buy everything. It makes my brain feel good, almost as good as pushing the buy-now button. The rule works this way: Put everything your heart desires in your cart. Wait 24 hours before you buy anything. Come back after 24 hours and decide what you really need versus what you want. Most of the time, I decide I don't need anything in the cart and then just close the window. This is a great way to separate yourself from the impulsive feeling of buying everything you want with a calm, cool, and collected mind that can later focus on what you actually need to buy. I've saved thousands of dollars with this trick over the years. Give it a try for a month and see how much money you save by tallying up what you would've spent versus what you did spend.

The Jar of Money Thoughts: I introduced this exercise to a friend a couple of years ago. She felt like she couldn't escape negative thoughts about money. These negative thoughts would tell her just to throw in the towel, that it was too late for her, and that she should just go spend money. I grabbed an inexpensive mason jar, and we sat down one day to write out new thoughts she could choose when all the negative ones started to rear their head. A few she chose were, "Money flows easily to me in all directions," "I've made good choices with my money," "I have everything I need right now," and "I am proud of all my ups and downs." You can feel free to borrow some of these money thoughts or create your own. What would you want money to say to you? How can you reframe some of those negative thoughts or moments that might lead to spending like there's no tomorrow?

The Jar of Money Thoughts has been a staple in my house since I lost my hearing. I think it's something that could really help you, too. It's an easy yet very effective way to retrain your brain around money and show yourself that you can be trusted. If a jar isn't your cup of tea, try journaling about a healthy money thought each day or write your-self a Post It note with your thoughts of the day and post it on your computer screen.

A Money Manifesto: You know how businesses will have a mis-sion statement or manifesto that they operate by? The same can be true of your relationship with money. Never heard of a manifesto?

Check out Apple's influential manifesto: "Here's to the crazy ones. The misfits. The rebels. The trouble-makers. The round pegs in the square holes. The ones who see things differently. They are not fond of rules, and they have no respect for the status quo. You can quote them, disagree with them, glorify, or vilify them. But the only thing you can't do is ignore them. Because they change things. They push the human race forward. And while some might see them as the crazy ones, we see genius. Because the people who think they are crazy enough to think they can change the world, are the ones who do."

Even if you don't love Apple's products, that manifesto is hard to pass up. A Money Manifesto is simply a written statement where you declare your intentions, motives, or views to yourself and anyone else who matters. You can be as verbose as you'd like or short, sweet, and to the point. Here's what I wrote for myself a few years ago. It hangs on my office wall, constantly reminding me how I want to interact with money.

This is the new way I'm choosing to do money. . .

I boldly opt out of the negative self-talk and thinking around money.

I celebrate self-worth over net worth.

I let my money tell the story of me, always being intentional.

I make my own money rules and define this thing called success.

I decide what a rich life truly is and walk freely in that direction.

I high-five progress over perfection because money is genuinely personal.

This is the battle cry for money's role in my life.

 TRY THIS...

Take a stab at writing a Money Manifesto that resonates with you. There are very few rules to this exercise other than making it feel true to you. You can write positive future statements like I wrote or use a more poetic style like Nike's manifesto. I encourage you to think about what your rules of conduct would be with money. How do you choose to spend and save your money? What do you value that you put your money toward? How do you want to interact or feel about money? What do you want to remember in those stressful moments?

I had a call with a friend the other day, and he said he had been thinking long and hard about his Money Manifesto. He'd gone through a big career change over the last year and was looking forward to reworking his rules around money. He went to his favorite restaurant, ordered a giant pepperoni pizza and a glass of Merlot, and let his mind wander. He shared that he scribbled notes on many paper napkins and ultimately landed on this as his Money Manifesto: "Worry has no place here. My money serves me and the ones I love with ease." A manifesto doesn't have to be long-winded or drawn out, it should simply mean something important to you.

As with all the Try This exercises in this book, work on this one somewhere that you feel inspired, like a coffee shop or your favorite park. Let your mind be creative and think outside of your current situation with money. You might be surprised at what you come up with!

THERE ARE NO RULES

There's a story in the money world that needs to be broken. Too many money experts want you to believe that you need to follow specific rules and a particular order of doing things to succeed in money. That's ridiculous. It's called personal finance for a reason. Money is personal, and you get to make the rules. You get to decide what works for you and what doesn't. You can choose if you want to have a baby, buy a house, get married, start a business, scrap it all, and retire early on a beach in Costa Rica, living The Pura Vida lifestyle. You get to decide what naughty money patterns to keep and which ones must be shown the door. At the end of the day, any money decision you make is yours. You can keep your money secrets under lock and key for as long as you'd like. Or maybe this chapter has inspired you to share a few secrets, which, who knows, could be fun.

If I were to offer you any kind of money rules that aren't *really* rules, these would be on the list:

1. Cultivate healthy and kind money thoughts and feelings. They dictate how you interact with money.
2. Get clear on your money values – what is important to you and what isn't.
3. Create an emergency savings fund with at least one month's worth of your expenses.
4. Create goals that matter and understand why they matter to you.
5. Figure out how much money you need each month to pay your bills, reach your goals, and have fun.
6. Create a spending plan that incorporates your goals and tracks your cash.
7. Pay off expensive credit card debt.
8. Invest as early as possible in your retirement plans and beyond.
9. Stay in your lane, and spend money that aligns with your values.
10. Don't compare yourself to anyone else. You don't know their backstory.

My yo-yo money pattern of spending money when I made more and penny-pinching when I didn't wasn't getting me anywhere. I was still in debt, miserable, angry at money, and operating in a far-from-ideal relationship with money. If I was going to live the rest of my life with single-sided deafness, I needed to embrace new patterns. It was the only way forward. Seven years later, I can tell you that I've made a lot of progress. It's so helpful to have some tools in the money toolkit to come back to, though.

Understanding your money patterns is important work. What motivates you to save and spend? What's going on in your life when you find yourself in a similar yo-yo pattern? What are the triggers that lead you to sacrifice your goals? It requires looking under the hood and pulling together all the lessons you've learned in this book: your money story, understanding money trauma, getting rid of money mistakes that don't serve you, clearing out old money goals and false beliefs, etc. You won't suddenly wake up with more money in your bank account. However, with a deep understanding of your past money patterns, you can start to build new patterns that will propel you forward in the future.

QUESTIONS TO PONDER

1. Would you classify yourself as a spender or saver, and why?
2. What is your go-to thing to splurge on, and why?
3. If someone dropped $10,000 into your bank account with no strings attached, how would you use it and why? (The answer to this question gives you clues to the action steps you should be taking with your money right now).
4. What's your biggest money secret that you've never shared with anyone before? What makes it so secretive? What are you afraid of if you were to share this secret with someone in your life?

CHAPTER **8**

What Is Your Money Happiness Number?

There's a money story in your head that needs to be shown the front door. It's the story that you can't be happy in life until you have a certain amount of money. That life doesn't begin until you log in to your bank account and see that magical combination of numbers. This money story in your head is robbing you of being your most authentic self. Imagine what it would feel like just to be you, a happy version of you, detached from the grip of defining your existence based on your bank account. Maybe I'm trying to create a magical land that just doesn't exist, but I'm determined to help you find money and happiness without losing yourself in the process.

Anne is one of those friends I wish I could hide in my pocket all day. I'd give anything to be able to pull out an Anne-ism from time to time to motivate me when I'm feeling down in the dumps. She has so many mic-drop moments when she speaks that I've lost count over the years. One of my favorite lines she shares that always makes me smile from ear to ear is, "Do not should on yourself." I, quite frankly, should on myself way too often. This is a work in progress you can hold me to.

Anne is a ride-or-die friend, always helping me through relationship issues, work issues, and, honestly, any issue that comes up in my life. There is *never* a subject off limits during a conversation about Anne. Something I find insanely refreshing in a true friend. One day, we were sitting and having lunch at our favorite spot and eating at our favorite table, doing what we call French Fry Fridays, when our conversation changed from gossip to money. We have laughed, cried, and everything in between at this little table in the corner of the restaurant we have lovingly named "our table." Anne usually shares pearls of wisdom each time we meet, but things were different this Friday. I asked her what her money happiness number was. This was the first time I'd ever seen Anne stop right in her tracks and not have an answer.

"What's that," she quickly replied. "Well, it's something I've been talking about for years, and it makes people think. We spend so much time working and worrying about paying our bills and getting ahead that we forget to figure out what will make us happy," I explained. Anne sat and pondered her answer over a few sweet potato french fries. She'd get ready to voice an answer and then pause, pull back, and continue thinking. "That's really an interesting question. I've never thought about money that way," she said, still in full-on thought mode. "Okay, let's say there is an amount of money that will pay all your bills, help you fund your money goals, and give you enough left over to pursue some of your passions, desires, interests, etc. That's the number you want to find. We all have a happiness number, but most of us have never figured out how to quantify that number officially. Forgetting what anyone else makes, has, desires, etc., when you have your happiness number met, to me, that is the starting place of financial freedom," I shared. "How many people are out there living their lives based on someone else's supposed happiness number and feeling entirely miserable in the process?" Anne shared. Exactly. I'd guess a lot of us. Me included. I believe that your money happiness number helps you stay in your own lane as much as possible and focus on how to use your money to create the life you want to live. It's a benchmark – a goal with which you can visibly align your money.

Over the next hour or so, Anne and I sat hunched over a plate of now-cold french fries and started to scribble down her happiness number on a paper napkin. It was a far smaller number than I might've guessed. This is one thing I admire about Anne. She can exist and be happy with very little money. She's had a lot in her life and gone through times when money was very lean, but she's never let money define who she is or steal her joy. That is a true gift, at least for someone like myself who has let money dominate almost the entirety of every thought that races through my head.

Your money happiness number is a place of extreme contentment. Whether that's $50,000, $100,000, or $500,000, when you reach your happiness number, your brain sends a message to your body that everything will be fine. You can relax a bit when you reach your money happiness number, or so you think. The problem is you can easily reach this number and then hyperfocus on why having more than this number should be the new goal. Thus starting an endless loop of always wanting and needing more to fulfill your happiness bucket. We aren't all meant to live in a big city with an expensive mortgage. We aren't all meant to be CEOs of companies and drive expensive cars. Conversely, we aren't all meant to live a simpler life in a yurt tucked into the wilderness or embrace the tiny living movement.

The amount of money you have does not define who you are as a person. This should be the motto that we all live by, but most of us don't. It is oh-so-easy to get swept up by what someone else has or appears to have and feel inferior. If you're learning anything from my story and the story of others in this book, it's that more of everything doesn't always equal a well-lived life. So, yes, knowing your money happiness number can *hopefully* keep you focused on your money and the vision you have for your life.

. . .

 MONEY TRUTH OR DARE

TRUTH: If you had one million dollars, what would you do with it?
DARE: Create a money folder with all of your important documents, including your life insurance policy, copies of your passport, Social Security card, etc.

. . .

WHAT IS HAPPY?

Here's something that might blow your mind. According to a *Purdue University study*, your tipping point for money, well-being, and happiness is reached when you earn $75,000. The study shows that earning more than $75,000 doesn't necessarily increase your happiness and satisfaction in life as you might think. Interestingly, it also found that you might experience a declined sense of well-being as you earn above that threshold. My professional guess is that when you hit that number, you start craving more money, increasing your expenses. The lifestyle creep, as we call it. You probably had some sort of reaction when you read this number in print. $75,000 feels like a dream for so many people, but it can also feel relatively low for others. This is the beauty of your money happiness number. It is unique to you; no one else gets a say in it.

The research is genuinely fascinating and such an interesting study of human nature. Maybe you've also heard that you need a million dollars to retire. Or two million. Or that making six figures means that you've somehow arrived in life. Or you should retire early, as all cool people do. We have so many beliefs that are never spoken but subconsciously control how we interact with money. So, what is your money happiness number? It sounds easy enough, doesn't it? And yet, this is the struggle that might be keeping you stuck. Getting to the bottom of your money happiness number will do a lot to help you, hopefully, stop panic-scrolling on social media, trying to fit into someone else's life.

You might also get stuck attaching yourself to someone else's happiness number and then you aren't proactive in taking the steps you need to reach your goals. I asked Amanda Holden, @dumpster-doggy and Investing Educator how you can break this habit of living someone else's happiness number. "I encourage people to investigate why they overspend. Is it because of boredom? Social comparison? On some level believing that this next thing will make you more loveable? A primal desire to be loved and to feel included are at the root of so many of our behaviors, including those to do with money. We all want to love and be loved. Friendships, relationships, and community are the great treasures of the human experience and essential to our survival. But we go about it all wrong! We attempt to back our way into love through a corn maze of personal success, money, beauty, and clout, instead of taking the more direct route of practicing love itself. This is a silly exercise, but think of the person you love the most. Do you love them because of their adherence to the (planet-crushing) trend cycle? Because they have the latest iPhone? Probably not. It is likely because they show up for you, allowing you to be your authentic self. I don't find it useful to tell someone to 'stop shopping,' but to instead consider truer methods of achieving what it is we really want, which is usually love and does not cost money."

THE *B* WORD

It's time we have a conversation about the big, bad, "b" word – *budget*. Alright, you can be honest with me. How much do you hate budgeting? Yeah, me, too. I get it; you put down numbers on a piece of paper with grand hopes, and it never works out how you think. At the end of the month, you look back at your budget and wonder what went wrong. How can all these numbers be wrong? And then you just say, well, forget it, I'm not doing that again, and you go on living life spending money in complete darkness. You might even see your budget as something that limits your ability to enjoy life and spend money. Here's a fact: How you've been taught to budget doesn't work. Here's why – you can put down any numbers on your budget, and those numbers can be a flat-out lie. Try me. If you have a budget, how much did you truthfully spend on shopping, going out to eat, gifts, or any other expense that gives you feel-good hormones? I can almost guarantee that whatever number you just told yourself is not the actual amount. Don't beat yourself up. We're all blissfully in the same boat floating down the "I'm never going to look at my bank account" river. Knowing your numbers is the only way, mathematically speaking, to understand your money flow. And to be able to fix it.

Sure, the expenses you have to pay, like your car payment and your mortgage, those numbers don't change month to month. It's your variable expenses where things get a little hairy. Those sneaky variable expenses that change monthly are to blame for the mind-blowing craziness being done to your budget. You can quote me on that!

. . .

YOUR RELATIONSHIP WITH MONEY IS. . .

. . .with Ethan Ho, CERTIFIED FINANCIAL PLANNER™ and CEO of Kālā Capital

Shannah: What would it be if you described your relationship to money as a Hawaiian island?

Ethan: If I were to describe my relationship with money as a Hawaiian island, it would definitely be Oahu. Oahu is known as the Gathering Island, and because I'm still in the accumulation phase of my life and I'm trying to gather dollars for my future, I think if I were to describe my relationship with money as a Hawaiian island, then Oahu makes sense. Also, as a financial advisor, I am trying to gather a community of like-minded individuals who want to embrace the positive side of dealing with money and their ability to use money as a tool to create their own unique rich feeling life. So from both of those perspectives, I would say Oahu describes my relationship with money at this time.

Shannah: What are your inner money thoughts or a central theme that plays on repeat?

Ethan: As a money expert, I feel like I should have my internal money thoughts under control, but I don't. I regularly feel and think that I am not living up to my earning potential, and financially, I am not where I want to be. I went through a whole internal or mental journey in my financial planning career where I had a lot of initial success and really didn't need to earn more money. If I maintained my trajectory, I would have more than what I needed, which was true, but after a few years of being stagnant and maintaining status quo, I found myself in a mental rut that ultimately came down to the questions of whether or not I was living up to my full potential. I realized that although I didn't need more money, I believed I was capable of earning more, and the thought that I was not living up to my full potential haunted me. I also believe that active income earned honestly is a reflection of the value we provide to the world, so if I was not living up to my earning potential, I would not be living up to my ability to contribute value to our world. So because I decided to chase my full earning potential and I delayed taking action, I regularly feel behind where I want to be and constantly question if I am maxing out my earning potential.

Shannah: What's a guilty money splurge that you are never giving up?

Ethan: Buying gear like surfboards is a splurge I never want to give up. Typically I find that people fall into one of two categories. They like to spend money on things, or they like to spend money on experiences. For me, I like to spend money on things that provide me an experience. Surfboards get me out in the water, in the sun, and exercising. They allow me to ride waves, which is something that really enhances my quality of life here in Hawaii. It's a thing I can buy once that will enable hundreds of unique experiences. I never want to give that up.

. . .

THE STORY OF YOUR NUMBERS

Claire and Paul had a classically messed up budget. They lived in a rent-controlled apartment in Los Angeles and had hired me to help them figure out what was going wrong. I came in, sat down on their retro 70s yellow velvet couch, and asked the question I asked anyone who had hired me, "Do you have a budget?" Paul reached over to his cluttered desk, ruffled through a stack of papers, and handed me a crumpled-up piece of paper they used as their monthly budget, which hadn't been touched or updated in years. There were a few coffee stains from months past and a small tear down the right corner of the page. "When was the last time you updated your budget," I asked. "Um, well, we don't update it. Why would we do that? We have all the numbers down here, and they stay the same pretty much every month," Paul shared. This was clue #1 for me that there was a disconnect between their numbers and reality.

Claire and Paul had a big goal of wanting to buy their first house, and in Los Angeles, which is an expensive proposition. They needed to save around $50,000 for their down payment, and when we met, they had only $5,000 saved. "Great, let's figure out how much you're spending and how much is enough for you both, and then we can work on figuring out how much you need to save each month to buy your house. Tell me, what's your favorite thing to spend money on," I asked. "We love to eat out and treat our friends, but we try to keep that to around $300 a month," Claire enthusiastically told me. "We just really can't figure out why our numbers never work. We both make good money, and our expenses are pretty low. It seems like all our friends are out there buying houses, and we're still stuck in this apartment spinning our wheels," they shared. I assured them I'd get to the bottom of the issue once I had a chance to review their bank statements.

Knowing there was more to the story than they were sharing, when I got home, I rifled through their bank statements (where all the money truths live); I was in shock and awe. They thought they were spending $300 a month eating out because that was the number on the crumpled-up piece of paper. Brace yourself; their monthly hefty food bill was, in reality, $3,000–$4,000. I scrubbed through the bank statements several times to ensure my calculations were correct. I threw my head back and smiled enthusiastically. I know when I find these hidden gems buried in someone's spending just how life-changing they can be. So, two things here. First, they had no idea they were spending that much because they never bothered to add up all the numbers. Second, this is the power of your brain on money. They had convinced themselves they were only spending $300 a month because they wrote it down on their crumpled-up budget. Yes, they repeatedly handed over their credit and debit cards to pay for dinner. Yes, they knew those meals were pricey. But no, they had no conscious awareness of the grand total each month. Nor did they care. . .that is, until they had a goal they were desperately trying to reach, like buying a house.

I asked them their favorite food item before setting up the follow-up meeting. This is a tactic I often use when delivering not-so-great news about people's money situation. Their reply was tacos from a little authentic taco shop that wasn't too far down the road from their apartment. Just before I arrived at their house, I stopped by the taco spot and ordered a gluttonous amount of tacos, complete with chips, queso, and homemade guacamole. I'm going to need it all to soften this blow. When I arrived, we sat and feasted on the delicious tacos and chatted about the latest gossip in the world. I was there for about an hour before Claire stood up and said, "Okay, I'm really curious: Do you bring tacos to all your follow-up meetings?" "No, but I wanted you to feel really happy before we talked about numbers," I said with a smile on my face. I pulled out their bank statements, all my notes, and a new and revised budget that I refer to as a Mindful Money Spending Plan. "Do you want the good or bad news first?" I asked. "Good news, please," said Paul. "Well, the good news is that you are going to be able to afford your house sooner than later, but the bad news is that you are going to really need to make some changes to your spending," I said. A look of panic and fear washed over their faces, afraid to ask any further details.

Seeing the reality of your numbers in black and white in front of you can be quite a shock. Claire and Paul sat motionless as I explained the diagnosis of their spending. Their eating-out numbers were getting in the way of saving for their house. That and a few other categories, but eating out was the main culprit. I explained how powerful your brain is when it comes to money. Commonly, you convince yourself how much money you are spending without knowing the truth, the actual numbers themselves. Spending money is a dopamine hit, and for this couple, their love of eating out overpowered any logic regarding the amount of money they were spending. We got down to basics, devised their money happiness number, and created a Mindful Spending Plan with a new and improved eating-out budget. They could still treat friends to dinner, but there had to be limitations around the amount they spent to reach their coveted goal of buying a house.

Seeing the numbers is just part of the equation. The second part, the most challenging part, is creating new patterns and behaviors or boundaries with your money. To remove their financial blind spot around eating out, we set up a special savings account where money flowed automatically each month. That savings account, called Let's Eat Out, would be the only amount of money they could spend each month on food. Once it was gone, they would have to wait until the following month to have the account replenished with funds. (Yes, of course, they could always spend more money if they really wanted to. But what I'm trying to do is set them up for success as best as I can. The rest is up to them.) I'm happy to report that after following their Mindful Money Spending Plan to a "t," they had enough money within eight months to buy their home. And yes, they still ate out a lot. More importantly, they learned how critical it was to track their spending until their money choices became easily repeatable patterns and behaviors.

. . .

 UNRAVELING THOUGHT #8

Your money happiness number is not up for negotiation with anyone but yourself. You get to decide what makes you happy and how much that lifestyle will cost.

. . .

MINDFUL MONEY SPENDING PLAN

I'm permitting you here and now to ditch your tired old budget and adopt a Mindful Money Spending Plan for yourself. There's just some-thing about the word *budget* that instantly can put you in a panic spiral, so let's just get rid of it. My one rule with money is that if the name of something makes you break out into cold sweats, change the name, but don't abandon the process. A Mindful Money Spending Plan puts you back in control of your money and is like a refresh to your brain. The word *mindful* comes in because this type of spending plan helps you pay close attention to what your money is doing and where you want it to go in the present moment. A spending plan puts you back in control of your money. It feels more aspirational than a budget. A spending plan isn't about telling what you can't spend money on. It's the opposite. A spend-ing plan tells you what you can spend money on and how to spend your money in a way that helps you reach your money goals. It's a refreshing approach to the old-school budgeting process – a mindset shift.

The Mindful Money Spending Plan tells your money what it can do. Think of it like a GPS for your money, directing it where to go and when to go there. Imagine if you were in Los Angeles and needed to drive to New York City. Just when you got ready to leave, someone told you there weren't any directions for getting there; you'd just have to figure it out on your own, without any GPS assistance. Pretty terrorizing, if you ask me. You might still get to New York City, but it will probably entail many twists and turns and take much longer than if you had the exact directions. This is the same feeling your money has when you don't give it direction.

The Mindful Money Spending Plan breaks the traditional budgeting rules *on purpose*. Instead of creating a single column of numbers at the beginning of each month only to fail disastrously, the Mindful Money Spending Plan follows a two-column format, looking backward and forward.

Column #1 – What I Think I Will Spend: You complete this column at the beginning of each month, and it estimates what you will spend that month. Think of this column as your traditional budget column. You list your income, fixed expenses, the stuff you have to pay each month, and your variable costs, the stuff you want to pay for each month. With this column, you are best-guessing what you think your numbers will be each month. Start by filling in the easy stuff like your income and fixed expenses such as rent/mortgage, car payment, student loan payment, groceries, insurance costs, minimum credit card payments, etc. These numbers likely do not change from month to month. Then, start your list of variable expenses such as eating out, shopping, entertainment, travel, gifts, etc. These numbers will vary from month to month, so you can use an average of what you've spent the last few months or just take a guess. You want to allocate every expense to a category and avoid a giant miscellaneous category. Every expense needs a home.

I'm breaking in here to explain a little insider secret to you about spending plans. Remember all those money goals you have? Make sure you create a line item for them on your spending plan. Each goal can have a separate line and a separate amount of money you want to "budget" for each month. I'm a big fan of breaking big goals down into micro-goals.

Micro-goals help train your brain to see the progress you are making, inch by inch. Let's say you aim to save $5,000 for a dream European trip to England. My first question to you is, "How important is this trip? What would it mean for you to be able to travel to Europe?" Having a strong WHY behind your goal is the motivation you need when you are stuck between choosing to spend your money on something at the moment that you really want versus deciding to save the money and put it toward your trip fund. The stronger your WHY is, the better your chances of making a decision that moves you closer to that goal.

Let's workshop this out a bit. Pretend that you said your *why* was something like this: "Going on this trip means everything to me. My family is from England, and I'll get to see all the sights my grandparents talked about over the years when I was young. I also work really hard and feel like I need a vacation to destress and get away for a while. When I return, I will be recharged and have some incredible new experiences to share." That feels like a pretty solid *why* if you ask me. Next, we need to make this goal of $5,000 a little bit easier for the brain to process. If you decide that you want to travel next year, that gives you 12 months to save, needing to put aside $416 a month into your trip savings category on your spending plan.

The next question to ask yourself is, "Is this savings goal doable in that timeframe?" This is where your Mindful Money Spending Plan becomes super-handy. Your plan will show you whether that goal is possible and will show you opportunities to make changes to your current level of spending so you can reach this goal. Rinse and repeat this process with all your other goals so you can accurately represent how much money you need to put aside each month.

For any annual expenses like your homeowner's insurance, car insurance, or health savings, you can break those expenses down into monthly savings targets. This is also known as sinking funds. Any expense that you pay semi-annually or annually works well for this type of savings approach so you make sure you have the amount of money you need when you need to pay the bill.

Alright, onto Column #2.

Column #2 – What I Did Spend: You complete this column at the end of each month; this is the truth bomb. This column is the reality check and represents what you spent during the month down to the very penny and the place where traditional budgets fall short and leave you high and dry. There are lots of ways to find these numbers. You can print off your bank statements like I did with Claire and Paul. Take out a couple of different colored highlighters and start organizing all your expenses into categories. These categories should then correspond to your spending plan document. There are also a lot of money apps that will automatically categorize your expenses. All you have to do is copy those numbers onto your spending plan each month. Some banking apps offer this type of categorization as well, making things really easy for you.

Once these numbers are laid out, compare and contrast the two monthly columns to get an accurate picture of how much and where your money is going. This, my friend, is a beautiful thing. From here, you've got two choices: (i) Great, I want to continue to spend this much for this category, or (ii) Yikes, no way, let me make some tweaks to spend closer to what I hoped I would spend. Once you have this information, you can figure out how much is enough to live your life monthly and yearly. This is the basis for your money happiness number.

▶ **TRY THIS...**

The beauty of creating a Mindful Money Spending Plan is you can uncover hidden amounts of money in your bank account and start using them differently. I've done this process with hundreds of people and haven't encountered anyone yet where we haven't found money hidden in their bank accounts. I'm talking about subscriptions you don't remember you have and don't need, fees you are being charged for things like your bank account and ATM fees, and any other expense you forgot you were paying for. They didn't need to earn more money; they just needed to figure out how to spend and save their money more mindfully.

As I mentioned above, go through the process of creating a two-column spending plan. Try it for the upcoming month so you can start fresh. When you get to the end of the month and start to compare and contrast what you thought you would spend versus what you did spend, highlight any amounts of money that are different. Let's go back to Claire and Paul as our example. Obviously, their eating-out numbers would be highlighted as a major red flag. There are a couple of things to think about in this situation.

1. Can you identify the reason why your actual number is higher than your projected number? Did you have a terrible month and find solace in eating

out with friends? Did you go on a trip and eat out more than usual? Or is this number the amount you spend most months? What's important here is not to shame or blame yourself for any money you spend. Trust me, this doesn't help the situation. You are just searching for the *why* behind the number so you can figure out what to do next. This is where your new thoughts and feelings come in.

2. Once you have a feel for why you are not okay spending this amount of money each month, come up with the amount of money that you are okay spending. That new number needs to go in column 1 of your spending plan next month. But this doesn't fix the behavior. That is, again, where the work comes in. There are lots of tricks to try. You can create a special savings account like Claire and Paul and force yourself to pay only for your eating-out costs from that account. You can set aside cash using the envelope method and train yourself to use the cash for those costs. This is where knowing yourself is crucial. How can you stay motivated? How do you work best? What will get you excited about this process? After all, these are your goals and not mine. They need to really matter to you, or your lazy brain will take over and stay in the comfy, albeit often scary, place, of how you spend your money.

It's a glorious day when you find these spending areas that don't align. Think of it as finding a lucky penny on the floor, heads side up. These mismatched areas of spending are opportunities for you to put your money to work mindfully. That extra $3,000 that Claire and Paul were spending – that money got re-routed toward their house savings account. We set it up as an auto debit from their bank account, so there wasn't a sneaky temptation to spend it. If we leave it to our own devices, we'll always choose to spend the money. Spending money is just a lot of fun and just feels so deliciously good.

This process can also work for chronic savers. You may be great at saving money but could be better at spending it. Please come over for a day and let me take your savings for a joyride. Kidding, of course. Saving money is excellent, to a point. It isn't serving you if you just leave money in your bank account. Your money isn't earning interest to keep up with inflation and can be better used toward your lifestyle and retirement goals. The only person happy in this scenario is your banker because they can earn interest on your money just sitting there hanging out. Yes, have a savings account. Yes, save money. But find the balance between a comfortable amount of savings and making your money work for you, aka growing your money and enjoying life.

The changes you must make with your money aren't as sweeping as you might think. You don't need to win the lotto or rob a bank. The best place to start is by determining how much is enough, knowing what your numbers are, and focusing on intentional spending. Add in a dash of positive thoughts and feelings around money, and you'll start to see opportunities to make the most out of what you've got. It's like having a secret money decoder ring. You truly can become your own money superhero.

QUESTIONS TO PONDER

1. How much is enough for you?
2. What would you be doing if you didn't have to work for money?
3. What short-term and long-term goals do you want to achieve?
4. What steps/changes are you willing to take to achieve your goals?

PART
III

How Can You Move Forward?

CHAPTER **9**

What Do You
Really Want?

"I need your help. I'm scared of money. I am so freaked out. I'm not sure you understand how terrorizing money is for me almost every second of the day, and I need to change that ASAP," Olivia cried out to me over our gourmet green smoothies in a small breakfast spot where we met early one morning. "Yes, actually I do. And to be honest, most people have some sort of the same feeling; they just don't talk about it openly," I replied, hoping to ease some of her anxiety. "Is there any fix? Any prescription? Or what about specific steps to take so I won't have these feelings about money anymore," she said, sipping aggressively on her smoothie.

Olivia's question was one I had thought about a lot over the years. What is the antidote to being scared of money? I had spent my entire life up to that point trying to figure this question out so I could help people navigate these fears. There are a couple of things that I know to be true. First, money is the giant elephant in the corner of the room. Even if you have a "good" relationship with money, money is always in the back of your mind. I hope to help you get to a place where you feel like you can openly talk about money, as Olivia did with me, so that money doesn't stay as much in the shadows as it does. The first antidote is just being able to talk about your fear, frustration, doubt, shame, guilt, etc., feelings about money. Giving your emotions a voice helps them become less powerful in your life.

Second, and this is equally important, you have to get really clear on what you want in life. This task seems simple, but it is much harder than it seems. When you unravel what you truly want in life, roadblocks can emerge. What would your family think if you wanted to live a life that didn't meet their expectations? What about if you are a woman and have always felt like you need to have a baby when deep down you are not sure that is what you really want? What if you took that job that pays really well, but you absolutely hate going to work every day, and now you are wondering if the paycheck is worth the pain?

I can feel the immediate pushback when I bring up this idea of getting clear on what you want in life. Common responses are things like, "I grew up thinking I could be and do anything in life, but here I am in my (fill in the blank age), and I realize that I can't live the version of life I want," or "What I want for my life is so vastly different from the day-to-day reality that I don't see any way to make it happen." I hear you, but just hold on to these thoughts longer without putting a lot of weight into them.

Olivia was a new client referred to me by a past client who had a total money transformation inside out when we worked together. Olivia's original request was to see if I could help her figure out how to get her money to support the life she lives. She was in her mid-30s, had a pretty good job with a multiple six-figure salary, and was tired of searching online for money advice that wasn't helping her. She got married a few years prior in a seriously romantic three-day wedding, and she and her husband were delightfully and blissfully in the honeymoon stage. Still, she admitted to me that they hadn't talked about money; beyond that, they were determined never to fight about money. This was the first warning sign that went off for me. Not talking about money doesn't mean your marriage is doomed. However, avoiding talking about money sets a tone that money is an off-limits conversation, which can work to support money beliefs you might've witnessed as a kid. For example, I vividly remember many situations when we would buy something with my mom, only to "sneak" the packages into the house without my dad seeing them. "Don't tell dad (or mom)" is a common money message many people receive. What this does as a kid is set the tone that talking about spending money or even bringing up the subject of money is off-limits.

Olivia and her husband kept separate checking accounts and would transfer money each month to a joint checking account for various house expenses. Beyond that, neither of them knew exactly how much money the other one had at any given time. Practically speaking, Olivia shared that she *should* always have enough money in her bank account, but things never worked out that way. She was always over budget and unable to contribute the amount she had promised to the joint account every month. There goes the wish of never fighting about money. Olivia felt depressed and overwhelmed by the stress of money. She was stuck in a belief cycle that she would never be able to reach her goals, even though she made a nice salary at work. She was in a place that you might recognize.

A couple more sips deep into our green smoothies, Olivia shared with me that she had a brain with racing thoughts and had tried to be better with her money, but she couldn't figure out how to do it. "It's like a complete mystery to me, and I can't seem to understand how other people have it figured out, and I don't. I walk around with this underlying shame all the time, thinking that I'm failing both my husband and myself," she said with tears in her eyes. "That's a lot to carry around every day. So tell me, what do you want?" I asked her. "What I really want is to have a money system that helps me move closer to my goals no matter how I feel. I can have emotional moments and spend a lot of money at one time, and that behavior destroys my progress over and over again. I want to figure out how to contribute to our house fund every month, have some money I can spend when I have an emotional moment, go on two trips a year, and start funding my retirement. That would feel like a success," she said.

. . .

 UNRAVELING THOUGHT # 9

A goal is just words written down on paper or imagined in your head until you put action, belief, and emotion behind it.

. . .

THE GOAL GAP

I refer to this gap between your current financial goals and your desired future as "the goal gap." It's really common, and I've experienced it many times. The frustrating part of the goal gap is that you begin to believe that money goals happen for other people because they must've figured out some secret science for which you haven't found the magic potion. Don't worry, this isn't true. What is true is that there are a few causes of financial problems that get in the way of making progress toward your goals. Let's discuss.

Problem #1 – Your relationship with money. I've written this book to help you with this problem. Money is emotionally charged, and it takes some degree of reprogramming of your old thoughts and feelings to turn them into healthy ones. Start now by replacing any negative thoughts you have about not reaching your goals with something affirmative like, "I'm taking action today that's going to help me reach my goals with ease." As always, put this in your own words.

Problem #2 – Lack of financial education. We've already talked about how dismal financial education is in the United States. In other countries, they're doing much better than we are here. However, most of us were never taught the basics of financial literacy – how to budget, save, invest, pay off debt, protect against financial risks, and create action steps to reach your goals. The good news is there are lots of resources out there to help you learn everything you want to know about money. Some of my favorite podcasts, besides *Everyone's Talkin' Money*, are *The Stacking Benjamins Show, Earn & Invest podcast, NerdWallet's Smart Money podcast, AffordAnything, BiggerPockets Money,* and *Catching Up to FI.* If you're looking for some good money books to supplement this one, I'd reach for *Happy Money* by Ken Honda, *The Soul of Money* by Lynne Twist, *Ask Questions, Save Money, Make More* by Matt Schulz, *The Simple Path to Wealth* by J L Collins, *The Psychology of Money* by Morgan Housel, *Finance for the People* by Paco De Leon, and *Happy Money, Happy Life* by Jason Vitug. These are all great resources to help you gain a deeper level of financial literacy.

Problem #3 – You need more money. This is a tricky problem with two solutions. One is to make more money. Easier said than done, I know. There are a couple of ways to tackle this problem. Ensure you are advocating for your worth at work or charging your clients a price comparable to your skills. No one else will if you don't advocate for a better salary. Know your worth, and don't be afraid to ask for it. You can also look at taking on a side hustle. Two great resources that are super-knowledgeable about side hustles are Whitney Hansen, host of *The Money Nerds* podcast, and *Side Hustle Pro* with Nicaila Matthews Okome. The second solution is to lower your expenses. It's a tough solution that can't be fixed easily. This is where deeply understanding your spending habits is incredibly helpful. If you're looking for some quick tips, here are some of my favorite ways to lower your expenses.

- Call your cell phone carrier and ask if you are on the best plan for your usage. Carriers always come out with new plans, so there is likely a better plan to save you money.
- The same goes for your internet company. Call and see if you're on the same plan or if you can bundle services to save money.
- Turn off the subscriptions you aren't using. I have a habit of signing up for those free trials and never canceling them. Don't be like me – cancel all the ones you aren't using. You can always sign up again.
- Call your credit card company and ask for an interest rate reduction. This isn't guaranteed, but it's worth the ask. If you lower your interest rate and carry debt on that card, you can pay off the balance more quickly.
- Shop around for your car insurance at least once a year. A guest on my podcast blew my mind when she said that car insurance rates are always in flux. Most of us get a policy and never even think about price shopping.
- Bundle, bundle, bundle. If you have renter's or homeowner's insurance, bundle that with your car insurance, and you'll save money. Ask for good driver discounts. Bundle your internet and phone service if you can.
- Ask about the perks at work. There are often hidden money-savings gems in your benefits package at work. Some companies offer discounts on gym memberships, travel, insurance plans, entertainment, continuing education, etc.
- Use a rewards credit card like a debit card – this means you pay off the balance every month but reap the rewards. I know credit cards get a bad rap. I understand. You should move along if you aren't good with credit cards. However, if you have a good relationship with credit cards, you can redeem all those points for lots of different expenses like airfare, hotels, car rental, cash back, and even gift cards for retailers and restaurants. Over the years, we've saved more than $20,000 (if not more) by using points for our travel expenses.

Problem #4 – You need to prepare for financial emergencies. Money surprises come up; sadly, they almost always cost more than you think. These little surprises can throw a monkey wrench into the progress toward your money goals. To fix this, the aim is to save three to six months' expenses in an emergency fund. Put your money in a savings account that earns a higher interest rate, like a High Yield Savings Account. Don't let the amount of money you need to save for your emergency fund freak you out. Save what you can when you can. Something is better than nothing.

Problem #5 – Your relationships. This might be a time to set some boundaries with your loved ones or have some of those tough money conversations that you've been avoiding. Get this: More than 3 in 5 US adults, 61%, have made a loan to a family member or a friend, and they'd rather let that money go unpaid versus asking for repayment. It's okay to ask your family members and friends for repayment and to set a boundary around how much and when you will support others. Also, we have to talk about financial abuse for a minute. Domestic financial abuse is rarely talked about but is unfortunately very common. Financial abuse is a form of control over the victim. It can show up in many different ways, such as sabotaging their employment, hiding money, assets, and debt, taking over the finances without a level of transparency, and coerced debt, where the abuser opens up credit lines with the victim's Social Security number. If you are currently in one of these situations, please seek help. There are national victim hotlines and shelters in almost every country that you can turn to for a safe haven. Do what you can to document the abuse that is happening, and please stay safe.

Problem #6 – You don't have a plan. Congrats, if this is where you're at, I've got you. Creating a spending plan is the first step toward reaching your goals. In a spending plan, you outline your fixed and variable expenses, as well as your goals, how much they cost, and when you want to achieve them. I know looking at your numbers can be scary. Hello, it took me years to look at my ATM receipts. I don't advise my approach. Remember, one of my most important rules is that your bank account balance does not determine your worth as a human!

. . .

 YOUR RELATIONSHIP WITH MONEY IS. . .

A conversation with Jessica Spangler, author of *Invest Like a Girl*

Shannah: If there was one money mistake you could get a do-over for, what would it be?

Jessica: I didn't find out until grad school that I could negotiate my scholarship. When I was deciding between a couple of pharmacy programs, I threw out an email to the dean explaining that I'd really love to accept, but the cost of attendance was important to me as I was managing the cost on my own. They doubled my scholarship.

Shannah: Take me into your inner thoughts about money. Is there a central thought or theme that plays on repeat?

Jessica: I grew up with an unrelenting scarcity mindset, and it took years to override that. My north star, for the longest time, was that I cannot rely on another person for income, I will not rely on another person for income, and that one source of income is only one step away from no source of income. To be frank, I still feel that way, but the context is different. Investing shifted my perspective from one of scarcity to one of abundance. I'm no longer afraid of what's to come, because I trust myself to take care of me. I look forward to more money in the future.

Shannah: If you woke up tomorrow and had unlimited funds to spend, where would be the first place you'd spend them?

Jessica: After the shock and panic wore off? Probably an estate planning attorney. I could only truly relax in my first-class, lie-flat seats to Italy.

. . .

SO, WHAT DO YOU WANT?

Most of us exist in a pit of negativity – always thinking about what we don't have and what is lacking or missing. To top it off, we live in a scarcity mindset–driven society that constantly reaffirms those beliefs. You are constantly being inundated by messages in society that work to reaffirm how underprepared you are financially and how you'll never be able to catch up. If you have ever watched a commercial about retiring, you'll get my point. There's language like, "Well, I know you feel like you're never going to be able to retire, and guess what? That's probably true. Unless you use our product or service, which will magically solve your issue." All your brain hears in this scenario is that you will never have enough money.

This scarcity mindset starts the overspending hamster wheel effect. You need to buy more stuff. You need to do more stuff. You need more time. You need more money. If you look at any of the most recent studies, you can easily see how more stuff is getting in the way of achieving your version of financial success. Americans have an absolute mountain of credit card debt – $1.129 trillion to be exact. Between credit card debt, the high cost of living virtually everywhere, student loan debt, the wage gap, etc., it is increasingly difficult to get ahead financially. I always feel like I've got the good little angel sitting on my right shoulder who whispers, "Look, you don't actually need any of this stuff to survive. You have a great life; just enjoy it, stuff-free." On my other shoulder, that bad angel is screaming, "Buy, buy, buy. You need it all. Who cares about what happens to you when you are 80 years old?" I swear, these two forces are playing a game of tug-of-war all day long.

. . .

 MONEY TRUTH OR DARE

TRUTH: Would you rather not have a debit or credit card, or never be able to tip someone again?
DARE: Take today as a no-spend day – instead, find three things in your house you can give away to someone in need.

. . .

GET SOME GOALS

First, you need to set some goals, but let's be real here: Money goals fall into the same category as New Year's resolutions. They are easy to set but oh, so hard to accomplish. There are a couple of scientific reasons why this happens.

1. **You've picked a goal that is too big.** I call these "shooting for the moon" goals. Listen, big goals are great, but your brain doesn't really know what to do with them. Try focusing on mini-goals instead. For example, if you have a goal to save $5K this year, while admirable, that goal might feel big to your

brain, and then your subconscious says, "Nah, you're never going to get there, so why try? Just go out and spend that money. That will feel so much better." And then you feel like shit because you can't reach your goal, and the cycle continues. What if you took that $5K goal and said, okay, that's $416 to save per month for a year, or roughly $13 a day. . .you can do that. A couple of things happen internally when you embrace the beauty of mini-goals. First, you start progressing toward your larger goal quicker, so you feel motivated to keep up the excellent work. Second, you feel accomplished and, dare I say, excited about your progress. You know what happens when you start to feel motivated and accomplished simultaneously? These feel-good feelings bleed over into other areas of life. You are beginning to reach goals that always felt off in the distance. What else could be possible now that you are inching closer to your bigger goals?

2. **The motivation, or *why*, is missing.** To get out of the messy money cycle, you have to do two things – (i) Go back to the Money Pie and understand how important your thoughts and feelings are in your ability to reach your goals, and (ii) Create a vision/mission for what you do want and attach a *why* that resonates. Let's work this out a bit. Why does saving $5K matter (or fill in the blank with whatever bigger goal you have right now)? Will it get you your dream trip where you can reconnect with your partner, a friend, or a family member, and you will come back completely relaxed without a care in the world? Will it help launch a business that will open up new revenue opportunities you can use however you want to pay down your student loans or fund your retirement and give you a sense of accomplishment? Will it help you buy a house or help your favorite charity? And why do those things matter? What feelings are you going after?

   The *why* needs to be strong enough for you to stay intentional each month and set up the right system to save $400. There are lots of fun ways to remember your *why* each day. You can cut out a few pictures or write a few words representing your *why* and post this page somewhere you look at every day. You can also record a voice memo and say something like this: "I want you to remember your *why* behind saving $400ish a month. You always wanted to go to Bali and soak your feet in the soil of your ancestors. You wanted to swim in unbelievably beautiful waters and meet healers and people from all around the world. This has been your dream for years, and now you are making it happen. You are choosing mindfully how to save and spend your money to make this dream a reality next year. Close your eyes and feel what it will feel like to be in Bali. Keep that feeling with you all day long." Of course, make this your own, but I've found that recording a voice memo in the third person does the trick. You're declaring this is the person you want to be. At the end of the day, find something that often reminds you of your *why* for each goal.

3. **You aren't *truly* ready for change, and that's okay**. Maybe you want to be better at saving money, but what you need to do to make that happen is not worth it yet to you. There's no shame in deciding that your goal feels too big and you can't find your *why*. Or your *why* isn't strong enough. Or the mini-goals you would need to reach don't excite you. This is probably one of the most generous offerings you can give yourself. It is a permission slip to put that goal to the side right now without shaming yourself because you can't reach it.

STAGES OF CHANGE

Just like Olivia, most of your money goals never get achieved. They are written down on random pieces of paper or shared out loud, but you just don't seem to make progress. Let's change that. To do so, I want to introduce you to the six stages of change, known as The Transtheoretical Model, introduced in the late 1970s by researchers James Prochaska and Carlo DiClemente. These stages can become a roadmap for helping you create real change, aka set and achieve your goals. Identifying which stage of change you are at is essential in your process of moving forward.

1. **Pre-Contemplation: Denial that a money issue exists.** As the name suggests, you deny that you have a money issue. At this stage, you can ask yourself, "Are there money issues I'm avoiding? Why am I avoiding them?"

2. **Contemplation: Conflicted over whether you want to make a change with money.** In this stage, you can focus on why you want to change. How will this ultimately change your financial situation and lifestyle in a good way? Also, what's keeping you stuck? As the name suggests, you are contemplating the outcome of the change and how it will impact your life.

3. **Preparation: You start making small changes with your money.** This stage isn't about big, sweeping changes. Just like mini-goals, you can also make mini-changes. You could check in on your investments or bank account, talk about money, listen to a podcast, read a book, etc. In this stage, you need some money affirmations to keep you positive. A good affirmation in this stage is, "Each day, I am making positive changes with my money."

4. **Action: You are taking daily steps and making changes toward your goals.** In this stage, having a money support system or mentor is essential to your progress, as is building rewards in your spending plan so you can celebrate small wins. I'm talking about small rewards like treating yourself to an ice cream or a matinee movie. You are doing the work at this stage.

5. **Maintenance:** You are continuing the momentum. This is a tricky stage because it's easy to get tempted by your money scripts and old money beliefs. Again, rewards are important, as well as creating some coping strategies like mindfulness exercises, meditation, vision boards, etc., to keep you focused on your goals. Keep doing what you are doing because you are doing it.

6. **Relapse:** This is your failure, it didn't work, "you suck at money" mentality moment. In this stage, you want to get down and dirty and work on those old money scripts. Write a true-versus-false list so you can get rid of your false money beliefs and see them for what they are. Ground again in your vision

and goals, and start setting some small micro-action steps so you can see success happening. Relapse is not a sign of weakness. It's a sign of humanness.

 TRY THIS...

Here's a little exercise to get off the rollercoaster of trying to reach your goals, only to give up a few months or weeks after you set them. I want you to write out three short-term goals (things you want to achieve in a year or less) and three long-term goals (things you want to achieve in a year or more). Next to each goal, I want you to clearly define your Why, How, When, and Where. For example, let's say your goal is to fund a dream vacation for you and your family, which will cost $6,000. That's a great goal, but it's not specific enough to motivate you to make the intentional choices you need to make with your money. Here's a better way to frame this goal: My family trip will cost $6,000, and we will take this trip six months from now. We're going to Hawaii, a place I always enjoyed as a child, and I can't wait to show my kids how amazing it is. We'll sip on virgin Pina Coladas, go to a luau, and eat tons of ice cream. I feel so proud of us for saving and making this trip happen. It will allow us to have memories with our kids that they will remember forever. We commit to saving $1,000 each month to make this trip possible. See how much better that FEELS? It's actionable, passionate, and connected in a way that excites you to do what you must to afford this trip. You can do this little exercise with all your goals, big and small. Make them come to life for you so you can visualize yourself achieving them. Alright, off you go . . . . write out your goals.

Short-Term Goals

Write out What, When, Where, Why, and How for each goal

1.

2.

3.

Long-Term Goals

Write out What, When, Where, Why, and How for each goal

1.

2.

3.

We've discussed how powerful your mind is regarding your money, thoughts, and feelings. Making the changes you need to achieve your goals requires doing something different, often uncomfortable actions. I decided a few months ago that I was going to set a goal of not buying any new clothes, shoes, or lifestyle-related items for at least a month and see how I felt. My motivation was both money motivated (I wanted to use any extra money we could save to fund our Roth IRA accounts), and emotionally motivated (I wanted to see if I could train myself to stop emotionally spending money on stuff I really didn't need. I'll tell you, the first few weeks were r-o-u-g-h. I had to pull my fingers from the keyboard whenever I felt the urge to search one of my favorite online sites to buy anything. But I did what I tell you to do — let the emotion come without trying to push it away. Acknowledge it for what it is, just an emotion, and remind myself that I don't have to scratch that itch if I don't want to. I also reminded myself that I had a goal, why it was important to me, and what my action plan was to reach it. After week two, the itch was less and less. I was surprised at how complete I felt, without needing to turn to shopping to ease my boredom and emotions. Fast-forward, it is now three and a half months since I set that goal, and I've committed to reaching six months. Not because I have to but because I want to. Who knows, by the time you read this book, I might have gone for a year without buying anything personal for myself. My point is the uncomfortable feelings that you feel will dissipate, I promise.

I shared my experiment with Olivia, and she gave it a try, too. She went four months without feeling the need to spend money emotionally. She put that money toward the trip she wanted to take with her husband and sent me a picture of them hiking in Machu Picchu and enjoying some time off in Peru. She and her husband finally had a money talk and she shared how terrible she felt that her money was in a bit of a mess. A few tears and some heated emotions were shed, but they both made it through. Their commitment going forward is to support each other in the best ways they can to reach their individual and combined money goals. This doesn't mean there won't be bumps in the road, or they will never go off course. It's life, after all. But, they have set themselves up for success and have worked hard to create a good relationship with money individually and as a couple.

QUESTIONS TO PONDER

1. What is getting in the way of you being able to achieve your money goals?
2. What are three short-term and three long-term goals that you have?
3. What are some action steps you can create to move closer to each goal on a daily, weekly, and monthly basis?
4. What is the *why* behind your goals and your vision? How will achieving these things make your life better? (Dig deep on this one.)

CHAPTER 10

What Are Your New Money Behaviors?

Chicken broth. If you were to take the six steps down the stairs into my garage right now, you'd find eight cartons of low-sodium chicken broth sitting on the shelf, just waiting to be devoured. We could probably feed the entire neighborhood with an endless supply of homemade chicken soup and still have a couple of cartons of chicken broth lurking in the garage. In fact, in the last 10 years, there has never been a time that I needed a little broth for a recipe, and an unopened carton of chicken broth was not on hand. I realize the absurdity of this statement.

Remember my husband, the Nightingale money identity? Chicken broth is a prime example of his need to ensure we safely have enough food to survive anything that might require some low-sodium chicken broth. If it were up to me, we'd have a quarter of a carton left in the fridge, and I'd probably never think about chicken broth until that fated day when I needed more than I had. So we negotiated. He can have three to four cartons of low-sodium chicken broth at any given time, and I promise to tell him whenever we're nearing the end of a carton.

Forming new behaviors around money will require you to step outside what feels "safe." Having such a backlog of stuff tests my desire to never spend more money than we need to at the grocery store. I'm famous for saying, "That costs how much?" and "Do we really need that?" These negative money statements have led to me rarely entering a grocery store. Of course, I can do the grocery shopping if needed and have for many years in my life. However, I know my money personality and how insane my brain can be around numbers. It's emotionally and practically easier if I don't do the grocery shopping in our family. However, I understand Jeff has a different relationship with money than mine. He enjoys going to five different grocery stores and sourcing the best deals while maintaining enough food to keep us fed. This is just one example of why dealing with money in relationships is so hard. No one *really* wants to compromise, and everyone thinks their way is the best. (P.S. You know where to find chicken broth if you ever need it.)

. . .

 MONEY TRUTH OR DARE

TRUTH: Would you rather win a lifetime supply of groceries or go on an all-expense-paid vacation every year for the rest of your life?
DARE: Create a plan to save one month's worth of expenses (break it down into small daily or weekly savings targets).

. . .

MONEY COMFORT ZONE

You can learn so much about your relationship with money by exploring your "money comfort zone." This is where, like it or not, you spend most of your waking hours. It's human nature. Your brain doesn't want to create change because that takes a substantial amount of work. So, you tend to make money decisions consistent with your money comfort zone. This is how you can repeat patterns, no matter how much money you make or have. When was the last time you tried something different with your money? Maybe you read a book, listened to a podcast, or asked your friends for advice. You collected the information and told yourself that on a set day, you would do something different for a change. Start to invest. Ask for a raise. Talk to your partner about money. Walk past your favorite store and not go inside. Get an email about a musician coming to town and not hit the buy-now button. Those are just a few examples of things you might want to do differently with your spending and saving. However, you know what happens. You end up making the same choice as before and getting really pissed at yourself that you did. Why is this happening again, you wonder.

So you've got to start cultivating a new money comfort zone by creating new behaviors.

First, you must start by asking yourself questions to shake off your current money comfort zone. Let's go back to the chicken broth and use that as an example to show you how this is done.

What are my current money thoughts (both positive and negative), and why am I thinking them? Jeff questioned why an obscene amount of chicken broth made him feel safe and how it quieted his money scarcity beliefs. I had to examine my thoughts about why it matters if we stockpile items and why I immediately view it as a bad way to spend money. This question requires honesty with yourself and not being afraid to examine your thoughts around money. It's really easy to get judgy with yourself, but a lot of freedom comes from allowing a thought to enter your brain, examining it, and then setting a new pattern by thinking a more reaffirming thought. Here's an example of my new and healthy thought pattern: "There's nothing wrong with having two extra cartons of chicken broth. You can simultaneously achieve your money goals and enjoy some yummy food that needs a little chicken broth."

How do those thoughts make you feel, and why? Things get real when you have to start unpacking your feelings. This is the hard part of unraveling your relationship with money because examining feelings can make you feel very vulnerable. Jeff realized that the feeling of safety of having chicken broth at his beck and call came from his upbringing of bouncing around from house to house and not feeling a sense of security. If he could hoard, I mean stock up on, things like chicken broth, that meant he was "secure." I felt out of control spending that much money on chicken broth, so it also tapped into my childhood beliefs that you never bought anything unless it was on sale and certainly didn't need two of everything.

What's one thing I can do today or this week to create a new behavior? Setting small, easily attainable money goals and action steps is the best recipe. Jeff saying he will stop buying chicken broth altogether won't work. Me saying I never need chicken broth on hand won't work, either. One small action step for us to take is to decide how much we're okay to stockpile to meet his needs and how much we can cut back on to meet my needs. Simple. Easy to do. Creates a new money behavior for us both that feels healthier. This may seem like a silly example, but I'm guessing you have your own version of the chicken broth situation in your relationship with money.

Almost every time I met a new client, I could recognize the look of defeat in their eyes. They were stuck in the money comfort zone and couldn't escape.

Jeremiah called me one Thursday afternoon, a day after listening to a podcast episode of mine where I was talking about money behaviors. He was on the phone, but I knew behind the scenes he had the look of defeat on his face. He had a confession to make. "Shannah, I've been a fan for a while now, but I must get something off my chest. I need you to help me with my money situation. I'm good, very good, at overspending, like a pro. I'm a healthcare worker who works hard and loves my job. I was able to climb out of more than $35,000 of student loan debt, but that was only a few years ago. Lately, I don't know what's happening. I'm just overspending everywhere, and I have a bunch of credit card debt, which I'm embarrassed to share," he said. I can't tell you the number of people who have shared a similar story with me, and they feel a sense of utter disappointment in themselves for paying off debt only to get back into debt. I asked Jeremiah if he could identify anything in his life that might be causing this to happen. I explained that we must get to the root cause of why he overspent so that we could create a new money behavior different from what he's tried before.

Jeremiah grew up with a single parent who struggled to make ends meet. His mom worked several jobs, and he spent many afternoons and evenings alone. He cooked most of his meals and always packed his lunch for school as a kid. He lived in a rather wealthy neighborhood and couldn't understand why his friends all had new clothes and shoes, and he was still wearing stuff from a few years ago that barely fit. He would ask his mom why they couldn't move to somewhere less expensive so they had more money to spare. He never got an answer, and so they lived there for many years, struggling. He'd get special treats on his birthday and a gift or two at Christmas, but he knew not to ask for anything new any other time of the year.

Jeremiah got a job when he was 14, and by the age of 18, he was a manager at a local restaurant, making more money than his mom. As far as he knew, his mom never had any credit card debt, and he stayed clear of credit cards until he got to college. In his sophomore year, he passed a little booth walking to the quad for a snack that said, Apply for a credit card, and you'll get a $25 gift card for Starbucks. He was a big fan of the caramel macchiatos, and $25 worth of free drinks was as good of a reason as he needed to get a credit card. A few months after he received the credit card in the mail, it sat quietly in his wallet. He never thought about the credit card. That was until he started dating Trevon, and he wanted to impress him by taking Trevon to his favorite restaurant near campus. Cuban food, he knew, would be the key to Trevon's heart. Jeremiah had enough cash to pay for the meal but decided to give his little piece of plastic a shot at paying for dinner. "That started it all for me. Emotionally spending more on my credit cards than I needed. If I had an emergency, I'd also put it on the credit card," he shared. Before he knew it, he had more than $15,000 in credit card debt.

Jeremiah worked hard and paid it off once he graduated and got his first big job, but when his mom passed away early in his 20s, he found himself overwhelmed by grief and depression. His credit card was his only solace. Jeremiah booked a few trips overseas to Japan and Australia to take his mind off losing his mom and spared no expense. He ordered the most expensive champagne, stayed in fancy hotels, and bought enough souvenirs to fill a small storage space. He lived, and it was expensive, and his credit card was there for it all. Every time he would pay off his credit cards, he'd be so proud of his achievement. He'd walk around with a straighter spine and confidence in his step. Then, something would come up, and he'd spend all over again. Sometimes, it was on necessary expenses, like when he got laid off from his six-figure job, and other times, it was on things he longed for, like his record collection of soulful tunes from Otis Redding, Stevie Wonder, and Aretha Franklin. This cycle continued for years until he dared to reach out to me. He shared with me that he recently sat on his luxury couch, which he bought on credit, and looked around his house in horror. He felt detached from all the stuff that filled his house. In the words of a memorable refrain from a Talking Heads song written by David Byrne, *this is not my beautiful house; this is not my beautiful wife.* He felt like a stranger in his own life.

Jeremiah went on to say, "I know I'm back in some sort of depression, and I've been having back pain for quite a while. My doctor said everything checks out, but I can't shake this belief that my physical ailments have something to do with my overspending and generally bad money behaviors." He was definitely on to something. Scientific studies have linked financial worries and anxiety to physical ailments like depression, headaches, stiff joints, arthritis, asthma, and other health-related issues. A study by a UK group of scientists found that "financial stress was most detrimental to biological health, although more research is needed to establish this for certain. This may be because this form of stress can invade many aspects of our lives, leading to family conflict, social exclusion, and even hunger or homelessness." This study found that 60% of people who were experiencing financial strain had a great risk of developing potentially serious health issues. It's possible that money issues might actually be making you sick without you realizing what is happening.

Since doing this work, I've become acutely aware of what is happening in my body during financial stress. My shoulders tend to get uncomfortably stiff, to the point where I have obsessive thoughts of jabbing something into them to release some of the pressure. I've had stomach issues for years and regularly suffer from a mild case of insomnia. I know by now that my shoulders and other issues are the body cues that I need to do what I can to relax and refocus my mind. Sometimes, you can't escape the financial stress or tough situations. I understand that there are very real money problems that are hard to move past and often life-changing moments involving money that feel soul-crushing.

I encouraged Jeremiah to reach out for therapeutic help to process the very real trauma of losing his mom and his dad at a young age. Together, he and I dug deep into his upbringing and the money messages he received. This is why I'm so passionate about the work I do. When I get to see someone like Jeremiah have an *aha* moment around money, it warms my soul.

After hours of talking, laughing, and crying, he realized that the cause of his yo-yo spending was a need to fill a hole he felt his entire life. Using his credit card, he could afford all the gifts he never got as a child. He didn't have to worry about being able to afford dinner and drinks with his friends. He'd just charge it and worry about the expense later. However, the downside of credit cards is the mounting interest rates. With the average rate of credit card interest soaring to 24%, that seemingly inconspicuous $50 dinner, left unpaid for months, can grow into a much larger number. For example, the average US credit card debt is around $6,800. If you took five years to pay off that debt, you'd pay more than $4,900 in interest, almost doubling your debt.

That's just a simple example of how detrimental credit card debt left unpaid can be. Now that the emotional work was done, it was time to move to the practical money steps to change his behavior. He disconnected his credit cards from any online shopping wallets and shredded his credit cards. He spent cash for 30 days at the grocery store and when he ate out to become aware of how much money he spent. He focused on positive money affirmations and noticed any moments when the twinge of needing to spend money with a credit card boiled to the surface. After years of being in and out of credit card debt, he finally felt like he had created a new money comfort zone. "Let's not kid ourselves; it was hard work," he said on our wrap-up call.

. . .

 YOUR RELATIONSHIP WITH MONEY IS. . .

A conversation with Amanda Holden, (@dumpster.doggy), Investing Educator

Shannah: If you had to describe your relationship to money as a cartoon character, who would it be?
Amanda: Pinky and the Brain. I see money as a path to personal power (benevolent of course!) and that's the Brain part of my relationship to money. But the other part of me — the Pinky part — remembers to hold my desires loosely and to love myself despite my relationship to money or power.

Shannah: What is one money secret you have that you don't share very often?
Amanda: I'm almost 40 and have a roommate!

I live in NYC and have a great apartment setup. It is called a railroad apartment, long and skinny like it's on railroad tracks. Mine is essentially two one-bedroom apartments connected only by a kitchen. So, my roommate and I only share a kitchen. We have separate bathrooms and entrances. Many people would think I'm too old not to have my own apartment, but I love it. We have as much privacy as we want – we both have doors to the kitchen – but we also get the perks of having a roommate, like half-price rent in NYC. For what amounts to basically having all my own space, I pay less in rent than anyone I know in NYC. I don't care that people think it's weird to have a roommate; I am an advocate for a return to communal living, creative uses of space, and having rent that never stresses me out. (Of course, it helps that I love the woman I live with.) Having relatively affordable rent allows me so much financial leeway. I am able to invest a ton of money and live a very fun life!

· · ·

Not everyone is an over spender, though. Heidi is an example of someone on the opposite end of the spectrum. She had trouble spending money. Heidi was in her late 30s when I met her at a women's networking event for entrepreneurs. She had started a well-known makeup line that was sold in all the stores and had stockpiled a lot of cash. I was mystified when Heidi contacted me and asked if we could talk about her money issues. I had to overcome my bias, thinking someone like Heidi surely did not need money coaching. We met at her stylish Venice Beach loft, and I was in awe of her home. It was funky and eclectic, with the most amazing kitchen I had ever seen. As someone who loves to bake, all I could think about was how badly I wanted to get my hands on her classic French-style oven and whip up a batch of my famous chocolate cupcakes.

Heidi ushered me into her back lounge and admitted that she was extremely nervous about talking with me. She pulled out a stack of papers and put them in front of me face down. "I'm going to show you my bank statements, but I want to warn you, I'm not great with my money. I don't know what to do with it, so it just sits in my bank account." I promised her I would be gentle and that everything we discussed was confidential. When I looked at her bank statements, I noticed a lot of cash sitting in a low-interest-bearing savings account, earning 0.02% annually. I'm talking millions of dollars.

Heidi had clearly been a powerhouse in her business, and she had a lot to show for herself. What struck me when we met was her shame and guilt about not knowing what to do with her money. She had been worried that if she hired someone to manage her money, they would steal from her, and she wouldn't recognize it until it was too late. But, her real fear was spending money. Heidi had saved virtually every dollar she had made; the only expenses she allowed herself to spend money on were her amazing house and a trip or two every year. Other than that, the money she earned sat still in her savings account, not keeping up with inflation. Now, there's nothing wrong with just saving your money. No crime there. However, Heidi's money wasn't working for her and growing her wealth. She was locked in her fears of spending money for her entire adult life. I pulled out a sheet of paper and wrote down the number in her savings account at the top of the page. "We are going to, theoretically, turn this into a bit of a game. Let's create some new rules and behaviors around this money that feel good to you. Let's go shopping with it," I told her.

My philosophy on building wealth is that you need to create multiple buckets of money, each with a separate purpose. One bucket is for your emergency fund, another for your retirement savings, another for your investment home or primary residence if owning a home makes sense, another for your safe money, like a CD or High-Yield Savings Account, another for stocks where you can be riskier with your money, and so on. These separate buckets grow at different interest rates. You can choose which bucket you will get it from whenever you need money. If the stock market is down, you could leave that bucket alone and pull money from another bucket.

Visually, Heidi and I created different buckets on that paper. We drew lines from her total amount of savings on the sheet of paper down to buckets I drew on the page. She put some of the money toward her savings, some were to be invested in a retirement account, some went to a brokerage account where she could pick stocks to invest in, some was set aside to buy a second property, and some went into a savings account that was called, "Heidi's Spend Without Regret" account. We created a roadmap for her to "spend" her money in a way that aligned with her values and goals and put her money to work. Over the course of six weeks, we set up each bucket, one a week, so Heidi could work through the emotions of divvying up her money. She wasn't losing any money in this process, but to her brain, she was in some serious, scary territory. She felt safe and secure keeping that big lump sum in her savings account and admitted to logging into her bank account often to check on her money. The new behavior that she was forming was allowing herself to spread out her money in a wise way so she could build sustainable wealth without feeling like she was recklessly spending her money.

. . .

UNRAVELING THOUGHT #10

Creating a new money behavior can feel as strange as trying to write your name with your non-dominant hand. Don't aim for 100% success on your first try. The quickest way to create a new money behavior is repetition until it feels like a new routine.

. . .

THE MONEY DATE

Getting married for the second time means you can break all the traditional rules. Jeff and I went on a pre-honeymoon to Paris about a week before we got married, and it was magical. Sitting outside at a cafe with a glass of champagne in hand on a rainy Paris afternoon, we had what would be our first money date. Talking about money with your partner is rough, especially when you both come with a fucked relationship with money. As we sat there, we both realized how important learning how to talk about money with each other would be in creating a healthy and loving marriage. Something that we both hadn't yet experienced. On that memorable money date, we implemented one of our favorite money rules: Don't ask, don't tell spending limit. We set a spending limit that was okay for both of us to spend without any questions or side-eye. We didn't need to sneak packages into the house or hide them from each other. Any amount we spent over our don't ask, don't tell limit needed to have a quick check-in. This spending tip is my #1 go-to suggestion for couples to keep the peace when spending money. You each can feel a sense of freedom to spend money however you wish, without criticism.

I introduced the money date concept to Darren and Jacqueline, who had hired me to help them figure out their retirement plan options. On paper, these two looked like they had it made. A great house, great neighborhood, cars to covet, purses, fabulous trips, you name it. But I know with money, what's under the hood is more important than what's on display. I quickly realized that they never had conversations about money. They never shared their fears and feelings, and they carried a lot of false belief baggage. Darren thought that he had to be flawless and keep it all together. Jacqueline thought she had to show up everywhere flaunting their money. These two illusions were killing them both. As with most of my money sessions, this was more of a therapy session. There were tears, shouting, name-calling, and other various child-like behaviors. So, I scrapped the retirement plan strategy for a while and gave them the rules for a money date. They limped through it for weeks until a light bulb went off for them both – the reason things were messy in all areas of their marriage was that they were living in fear of who they would be if they didn't have money to show as a sign of success. And so they never talked about money . . . until now.

The money date is one of the best tricks in the book to bring down the temperature as a couple; however, you don't have to be in a relationship to have a successful money date. It also works great solo and is a great way to create new money behaviors. There are a few loose rules to money date success:

1. Calendar a date and time every week just like you do other appointments to make it a priority.
2. Go to someplace you love, like a coffee shop, a favorite corner in your house, or the park. Make it an enjoyable experience.
3. Grab a beverage and a few snacks and treat it like a date.
4. Your tasks – Review your spending the previous week or month and see if you want to make any tweaks. Then, review the

upcoming week or month . . . anything you need to change? Finally, review your goals and track your progress. Are there any new goals you want to set? This is the time to inventory what is going on with your money.

5. Use this time as an open, honest, and non-judgmental space to discuss or explore any thoughts and feelings around money piled up during the week or month.

6. Reward yourself for a successful money date. I'm a fan of going for a scoop of my favorite gelato. Make it small, but make it something you love. This helps tell your brain that you can be trusted to manage your money, and you should keep it up.

One of my favorite psychological tricks that I've used time and time again to form new money behaviors is to give myself rules of engagement around money. For example, I tell myself, "Okay, you have from 10:00 am to 10:15 am to think and feel any way toward money." Once 10:15 comes, I shift and allow my brain to think about anything except my doom-and-gloom money thoughts. You deliberately tell your brain when it's allowed to think and ruminate about money, when it's done, and when it's time to pack it in for the day. It's a gentle way to remind your brain and body that you control your thoughts and feelings around money and not the other way around.

Even with the best intentions, it can take time to create new money behaviors. I asked Joe Saul-Sehy, host of *The Stacking Benjamins Show,* what he thinks gets in the way of forming new money behaviors. "I think we clog our brains with the wrong messaging. We're too passive about what goes in, so advertisers and tech companies fill the void. It's easier than ever to be passive now. Netflix helps us be passive. TikTok helps us be passive. So decide to pursue what you want actively. We also forget how important it is to surround ourselves with the right people. When we moved to Texarkana, I had zero interest in running a marathon. Then, I fell in with a group of runners. Now I've run eleven of them, on top of some 100k bike rides, many 5k, 10k, and half marathons. The only reason I did these was because of my friends. It's the same with money. Fill your time with people who uplift you and who are already further on their money journey than you. You're certain then to create new money behaviors," he shared.

When creating new money behaviors, the goal is to have them become habits so you'll automatically follow through. These new money habits become a part of your daily, weekly, and monthly routine, like showering and getting dressed. The key is creating money behaviors you can easily follow through on. So many digital apps on the market can help you with this process and make it easy. Joe agrees: "Automate easy tasks like saving monthly or paying the minimum on your bills. Now you've freed your mind to think about new behaviors. Then, use your calendar and 'fence' off enough time to help you develop the new habit. Gamify the behavior. Celebrate small wins. Make it fun, and you'll be more likely to succeed." This is solid advice, my friend.

QUESTIONS TO PONDER

1. What new money behavior are you committing to adopt in the next 30 days?
2. What does a healthy relationship with money look like to you?
3. How do you want to feel about your money on a daily basis? And, do you believe it's possible to feel this way?
4. What ritual can you create to initiate weekly money dates? For example, packing a picnic and going to your favorite park, lighting your go-to candle, dancing your butt off to your favorite album, scream-crying to your favorite movie to get out all your feelings, or taking a walk around your neighborhood. A good ritual is anything that is (i) legal and (ii) makes you feel good.

CHAPTER **11**

How to Keep
Your Relationship
with Money
Unraveled

My favorite possession, undoubtedly, is my 10-plus-year-old blanket, which I lovingly call Blankie. Blankie used to be shiny, bright yellow, snuggly soft, and ultra-fluffy, but the poor thing has warped into the nastiest mustard color you've ever seen and lost almost all of its fluff. But I don't care. Blankie is my comfort, protection, and go-to whenever I feel terrible about my relationship with money or anything in life, if I'm honest.

I've panic-screamed into Blankie, drug Blankie with me around the world when I travel, cried into Blankie, laughed with Blankie, and wrapped myself up in Blankie whenever I want to feel like a kid again without all the adult-sized worries. Why in the world does a 40-something-year-old woman need a Blankie, you ask? Well, Blankie is my trinket, the thing I can touch and feel that reminds me that everything will be okay. No matter what money mistakes I've made, no matter how much (or how little) I have in my bank account, it's okay, and no matter how fucked my thoughts and feelings are around money, Blankie's there for me.

Listen, you can't have Blankie because she's mine, but I recommend finding something that gives you the same joyous comfort and irrational sense of joy that you can cling to. Having a trinket, something you can hold, smush, cling to, look at, feel, etc., is a child-like obsession that is okay in my book because dealing with life's financial ups and downs is not so easy. Anyone who tells you otherwise is straight out lying to your face. Money comes and goes. Things in life happen that you did not expect were going to happen. This is just the deal we make as a part of the human experience. It can be scary and exciting at the same time. One of my therapist's favorite sayings is that two things can be true simultaneously. You can be smart and still struggle with your relationship with money. You can have a lot of money and not feel happy at the same time. You can be so passionate about a business idea that you want to launch it and be terrified at the same time. Like my Blankie, you can hug your trinket tightly in the comfort of your home and still be brave when facing the outside world.

After I got divorced, I battled with my demons as a money expert. I had walked away from my home, virtually all of my possessions, and was starting over from scratch in my 30s. This was not the perfectly scripted version of life that I thought would happen. I would take my expensive dream machine car for a ride down Topanga Canyon to Malibu and park alongside the road at Zuma Beach to have some time to think. I kept a notebook with me and forced myself to write out my feelings in raw detail. I recently found that notebook and read over pages and entries titled, "Who the hell are you to give money advice? You are starting over from zero." It took me many years of working with a therapist and talking with my incredibly supportive friends to realize that I am exactly the *right* person to give money advice.

I'm learning how to embrace this idea of two things being true simultaneously. It feels like a pathway to letting go of a lot of money thoughts and feelings that aren't helpful. Your trinket, or comfort item, can be anything you wish, but I advise finding something that feels safe and doesn't harm yourself or anyone else. Countless people have threatened to get rid of Blankie one day when I turn my back, but secretly, they all know how much joy Blankie brings into my life and how vengeful I might be if they made me part with my emotional support Blankie! The point is that we all have deeply woven feelings about money; ultimately, we're all just trying to do our best to work through those.

. . .

MONEY TRUTH OR DARE

TRUTH: What money lie are you holding onto that you need to let go of?
DARE: Call your internet and cell phone providers and ask them is there a better rate available than the plan you are currently on. (Bonus points — if you end up saving money, move that excess amount toward one of your money goals.)

. . .

WE NEED TO TALK ABOUT SHAME

Shame is the deep-seated feeling about money that most of us share. When I think back to all the different people I've worked with over the years, there was always a deep sense of shame in how they interacted with money. It makes sense because the feeling of shame shapes our perception of ourselves and others and is central to our behaviors and decision-making. There are so many ways that shame can show up in your relationship with money and hinder your progress toward your goals.

Shame that you might not be where you want to be financially.

Shame that you made a mistake with your money that might have set you back.

Shame that you didn't start to invest early on and take advantage of the wonderful powers of compound interest. Now, you're in a panic scramble to make up for lost time.

Shame that you spent too much money traveling when you had other money goals, like paying off debt, that were more "financially responsible" goals. This comparison trap can suck the joy right out of you.

Shame that you don't have as much money as your sibling, parents, or best friends.

Shame that you have a really good job that pays well, but you feel like your soul is getting sucked out of you minute by minute every time you go to work.

Shame that you aren't able to give as much money as you'd like to your favorite charities. You ache to be more helpful financially.

Shame that you don't have money all figured out by now. If only you would've had access to the money playbook earlier on.

Shame that you have a lot of money and other people don't (yes, this is a real feeling of shame).

Shame that you should've known what to do with your money the minute you graduated college and not taken on all that debt.

At the core, the feeling of shame is about the desire to belong and be accepted as a good person doing good things. Belonging to something bigger than yourself is a big part of being human and a vital need we all share. However, shame does not have to keep you stuck, particularly with your relationship with money. Letting go of toxic shame and embracing shame for the teacher that it is will help ease your nervous system and will do a lot to spur on some of those good money thoughts that will move you forward. Your feelings of shame are like little alarm bells that go off from time to time, trying to tell you something that needs to be addressed. Before you think shame is all about telling what is wrong, hear me out.

Let's take a classic example that you might be able to relate to. Shame that you aren't where you want to be financially. First, this is a very valid feeling, as are all your feelings around money. I can't tell you how many people I've worked with over the years, all of different ages, demographics, income levels, etc., who have held this shameful belief that they aren't where they want to be financially. Thinking back about your Happiness Number, you can see the importance of defining this for yourself. If you don't truly know the number that will make you happy, pay your bills, and help you create a well-lived life, then you are always searching for more. My client Jeremiah was making more than a million dollars a year in a very lucrative career but couldn't shake the shame of feeling like he should be further in his career. He was stuck in a pattern of lifestyle creep, living a lifestyle above his means because he had told himself that this flashy lifestyle could cover up his shame. When we met, what he wanted was permission to take a lower-paying job with a company that he felt more closely aligned with. But how would he live with the shame of feeling further away from his mega-salary? He worked on his relationship with money for almost a year with me and finally got to where he said, "I think I finally understand my shame. How can someone with a large salary dare to wish for less? My family struggled for years, so I held the weight of them all on my shoulders. I realize that I can be happy with less and in fact, really happy. And I no longer have to carry this shameful feeling around. My life is for me, and I need to live it that way," he proclaimed after his revelation.

When shame is present, you intuitively sense a gap between where you are and where you want to be. This is a good thing. You can use this gap to open up a new frame of thinking. Instead of thinking, "I'm a failure because I haven't reached my money goals or don't have the exact amount of money in my bank account that I would like to," why not try a new thought like, "Look at all the things I have achieved financially. I'm pretty good at money." You might think, "But I don't believe that thought." *Yet*, this is the word I want you to try on for size.

You don't believe that thought *yet*, but you're opening yourself up to transforming your relationship with money and shame.

Shame is meant to be your teacher, not your punisher. The gap between what you want and reality can help you start thinking proactively about your situation and what you need to do to move out of shame. Are there money steps you can take right now that help you soothe this feeling of shame? Is there a money mistake you've made that you must let go of? Is there something financially in your life that you need to change? What is the truth behind the divide between where you want to be financially and where you are currently?

KICK SHAME TO THE CURB

I love helping people with their money, especially those just starting their careers. I met Naomi when she was 27 years old and in her first few years as a data scientist at a very large company. At our first money meeting, I was surprised at how financially together she was. It was a head-scratcher moment because I wasn't entirely sure why she needed my help. She had her money exquisitely documented in Excel spreadsheet upon Excel spreadsheet and cross-referenced in a popular budgeting program. All her numbers were color-coded, and each spreadsheet had its legend and notes section for reference. This type of detail is a level of sophistication with finances that I rarely see. But don't let all these fancy spreadsheets fool you into thinking that Naomi had a good relationship with money.

Naomi grew up in a family where the motto was, "We only buy things that are on sale, and anything we buy must be a good deal." Her father put this sentiment in place, and no one in the family dared to rock that boat. Yes, buying things on sale that are a deal is a great way to save money that you can use for other money goals. That is not what we're talking about here. The message received by Naomi was that you don't spend money on anything other than your primary expenses and things like saving for retirement and paying off your student loans and credit card debt. Money should not be used for fun or to make you feel good. She carried around this belief, influencing every decision she made about money.

In addition, Naomi watched the interaction between her parents around money growing up and saw that often, her mom did not have enough money to buy essential items she needed, like daily necessities around the house. Naomi felt a sense of responsibility not only for her finances but also for others around her. She always needed enough money to pay for any expenses her mom or other family members could not. This was a heavy burden and responsibility that Naomi lived with day in and day out.

I quickly realized that Naomi did not need help figuring out how much she had or where it was going like most people looking for money help. Instead, she needed help escaping the deep-down shame she felt every time she spent money on something that wasn't a practical expense or something that wasn't on sale. She felt paralyzed about spending money on extracurricular activities that would enrich her life, like attending a workout class or signing up for a workshop on pottery or photography. Naomi longed to live a more balanced life between work and play, earning money and having fun. She shared that she has never allowed herself to have fun if it meant that she has to spend money. Those purchases have always felt like she was throwing away money that could go to better use. What would her family think if she chose to spend money in such a "reckless" way? Instead, she internalized the feeling of shame whenever she even thought about spending money on something outside of that framework.

I asked her the same question that I have asked you to ponder through the pages of this book. "What do you want your relationship with money to look like?" I said. "What do you mean? I'm not sure I understand what you are asking me," she gently replied. "You have been living with a relationship with money that your parents have set out before you. But that doesn't mean their relationship with money is what you want going forward. You have a choice in the matter. You get to make the rules that you live by going forward," I shared.

Digging deeper, Naomi had a healthy emergency fund and was on her way to saving six months' worth of expenses within a year. (The classic money advice is to save three to six months of expenses; if you are a freelancer or run your own business, you should aim to save around 9–12 months). I feared she would never feel like spending her emergency fund savings based on her current relationship with money. And, when she did spend her savings, she would shame herself into believing she did something wrong.

Naomi expressed to me that she had been feeling sad and depressed lately and had probably spent too much money on her credit card in the previous months. So she found herself transferring money from her emergency fund over to her checking account to pay off her credit cards every month. This brought up a lot of shame and regret that she couldn't shake. A big part of redefining your relationship with money is learning to acknowledge these feelings for what they are: just feelings. They don't have to move you into a bucket of thinking that you are a terrible person and whatever other trainwreck sort of thinking that occurs. "Hey, why don't we set up some rules that feel good to you around your emergency fund savings," I suggested. "I've never thought about that. Can I really do that?" Naomi asked.

 TRY THIS...

This is a fun journal-style exercise to get you started thinking about what you want your relationship with money to be going forward. Get a fresh piece of paper, start a new document on your computer, or open the notes app on your phone. On one side of the paper, or at the top of your document, write out what your old, it doesn't work for me any longer, relationship with money looked like. Dive deep, and don't be afraid to get out all the nasty bits on paper. You can use my list to spur your thinking. Get it all out on paper, though. For me, this looked like:

- Perfectionist thinking and always having to make the right decision with money
- Being super-competitive with people, especially online, that I have to achieve what they have
- Thinking I need all the stuff, and expensive stuff, to be worthy of being me
- Feeling a deep sense of embarrassment that I'm a money expert and have still made a lot of really big money mistakes
- Shame, fear, guilt, and a general anxious feeling around money all the time
- Obsessive thoughts about money and a general inability to just fucking relax
- Working all the time to prove my worth and believing that working all the time will somehow bring in more money
- Not trusting myself and *really* knowing my worth
- Charging less than I deserve to get paid because that's the right thing to do

Step two of this exercise is to turn the page over, metaphorically and practically, and write out the new rules for your relationship with money. If the idea of rules seems too specific, think about the thoughts and feelings you want to embrace going forward. You can also borrow what you wrote for the exercise: "If money showed up at your door, what would you want it to say to you?" Here are a few highlights from my list:

- Embracing the present moment of what is and letting go of what was
- A deep sense of gratitude for where money has taken me
- Permission to spend money to feel good, with intention
- Allow me to have other thoughts than money
- I will choose a thought that is affirming rather than destructive
- Being super-content with the money decisions I make – guilt and shame don't belong here
- Remembering that everyone is on their own journey, just live my life and do it well
- My self-worth does not equal my net worth
- It's okay to buy things that aren't on sale from time to time
- Enjoy spending money on things like vacations and eating out – really just enjoy it

Take this exercise and make it your own. Once you have new guidelines that define your relationship with money going forward, rewrite them on a fresh page. This is the piece of paper that you want to keep handy. In any moments when you start to sense those feelings of shame, guilt, anxiety, fear, and so many others, take out your relationship with money rules and remind yourself how you are choosing to move forward. Your brain will beckon you to return to your old, more comfy relationship with money. Just remind it, "Brain, not this time. I'm choosing a new path going forward!"

Since Naomi is a spreadsheet woman, I encouraged her to write her money rules on each spreadsheet so she would remember how she wanted to interact with money. If you love a good Post It note, write down a few bullet points you want to remember about money and keep that note on your computer or desk when you are working. If you love the notes app on your phone, create a pinned note you read every morning and night. If you love a good whiteboard, write out your relationship-with-money pact on the board. These are your money rules – make them matter.

. . .

 UNRAVELING THOUGHT # 11

You have permission to opt out of all the negative self-talk and thinking around money and embrace a relationship with money that makes you feel good.

. . .

. . .

YOUR RELATIONSHIP WITH MONEY IS. . .

with Ellyce Fulmore, CEO of Queerd Co. and best-selling author of *Keeping Finance Personal*

Shannah: What would you say is your biggest money secret?

Ellyce: Ooh, a money secret. When I first incorporated, my business finances were a complete mess, and I am still working on correcting that. Many people assume because I am a financial educator, that I would have everything all organized. But my business blew up so quickly that I didn't have the capacity at the time to research options and set up automations. I'm still working on ironing out some of the issues that stemmed from that disorganization. I've never really talked about this, but I think it's important to share these challenges because starting a business is hard.

Shannah: If you were to describe your relationship to money as a cartoon character, who would it be?

Ellyce: The one that's coming to my mind is Joe, the animated character in the movie *Soul*, in which he embarks on a journey of trying to figure out who he is and what his purpose is in life. Joe ends up realizing that he prioritized his ambition over his own happiness. I feel like that movie kind of represents my journey of feeling the pressure of what I "should" be doing with my career and my money, and grappling with the fact that I wasn't fulfilled after achieving certain milestones. But through the process of exploring who I am and what success means to me, I came to the conclusion that I just need to do things my way. My money journey was similar to what Joe experienced in *Soul*, going from a lost soul to being filled with purpose, and that's where I'm at in my relationship with money now.

. . .

ONWARD

Like Naomi and so many other stories I've shared in this book, you've brilliantly survived all your hardest days to date and are still here. I want you to remind yourself of everything you've been through. Be your own coach. You have made it through all your money situations, the good and the not-so-good. My goal for you in this next chapter of your relationship with money is to go from surviving to thriving.

I know it sounds a bit cliche, but thriving does not have to mean that you make a lot more money or win a jackpot in Las Vegas. Thriving in your relationship with money is about learning to put money in its place. It's money. It helps you live life. It does not define who you are. And money cannot stop you from having a life well-lived.

Your relationship with money is the longest relationship you'll ever have with anyone. Anyone. Money is just a piece of paper or a coin at its genesis. It's a thing. Money is a tool to help you reach your goals, but that's where money has to stop. You get to decide how you think, act, and feel about money from this point going forward. You might not have felt in control in the past, but you've gotta know you're in control now. The choice is yours.

Keeping your relationship with money unraveled also allows for a healthy few minutes of panic when something isn't going your way. Cue the Blankie. My advice is to give yourself five to ten solid minutes to freak the fuck out at any time during the day. Then, get resourceful and make mindful choices with what you have available. This is good advice, even in the best of circumstances.

I've shared many exercises in this book, and I hope you decide to try a few. If you only take away one message from this book, I want you to remember that your emotions about money are real. Your brain and body recognize them well by this time in your life, and you don't have to be in an unfavorable financial situation to feel these emotions. This is the part of money we don't discuss often and part of the movement I'm trying to start. Strong emotions like anger, fear, guilt, shame, and judgment are prevalent in even the best financial situations. I want you to be able to embrace your thoughts and feelings about money and understand the role they play in your money journey. If you haven't guessed so already, it is the secret sauce; I'm convinced of it. We should teach kids how to make a budget, save money, and give to others, but also how to work through the windy road of money thoughts and feelings that bubble up to the surface. Money success isn't just about the numbers but also about what is going on in your brain and body.

The classic book *Think and Grow Rich*, released in 1937 by Napoleon Hill, is revered as one of the great books on money, self-development, and the power of your thoughts. Yes, the book can come across as very tone-deaf and sexist, but it was written so many years ago, so you need to read it with a grain of salt. The message, however, is what you can take away from reading the book. After talking with several individuals who had amassed financial fortunes, Napoleon wrote "13 Steps to Riches." Many of these steps still hold true today, such as the Power of the Master Mind, Organized Planning, and The Brain. While thinking good thoughts alone won't keep your money unraveled, it's a pretty good starting place to create change.

WHERE TO NOW?

After you've read this book, I want to be a purveyor of hope for you. I want you to feel like you can jump in the driver's seat and take control of your money journey going forward. There are so many voices out there trying to tear you down. There are a lot of very unfair money rules and practices that you might also be battling. I wish I could plant a magical tree in your front yard that would supply you with endless money and a ticket to a magical world where you never have to worry about money again. I hope that by reading this book, you are inspired to work on your relationship with money going forward. Maybe you can forgive yourself for everything you should've done with your money and let that stuff go. Maybe you can encourage yourself to create new rules for engaging with money. Maybe you will allow yourself to spend money on things that fill you up and bring you joy. Maybe you will go after a dream you've held onto but have been too afraid to chase because of money. No matter what journey you take from here, I want you to promise me that money won't define who you are and your contribution to this world. We all need you to be the best you.

Lastly, memorize these five key takeaways. They will serve you well and help you keep your relationship with money unraveled.

#1 Your thoughts and feelings around money set the tone for everything. They influence your action steps and, ultimately, define your money habits. You don't need good money thoughts 100% of the time. That is just impossible. Instead, aim for 70–80% of the time. More than anything, remember that you can choose what to think. Your first thought is usually somewhat (or always) negative.

That's okay. Choose a better second and third thought and see how it changes how you interact with and feel about money.

#2 Don't hyperfocus on how much money you save. Instead, focus on how you are spending your money. Track your money and understand how and where you are spending it. Make intentional spending choices that move you closer to your goals. Build rewards and feel-good money into your spending plan. Set your money flow up on automatic withdrawals so you can send it to all the places you need and want it to go without making a conscious decision every time you spend money. And, lastly, just do the best you can.

#3 Release the feelings around money that keep you locked in shame. Let go of your money mistakes. Trust me, you'll make plenty of them. We all do. Focus on what is going right. Those are the things to celebrate. If you find yourself in debt, don't punish yourself. Instead, think about how your debt has helped you (even if it feels weird). This might seem counterintuitive, but maybe your debt has put a roof over your head, fed your family, or helped your business stay afloat. If you feel like you're not good with money, look for validation that you are good with money. You've read this book . . . that's a solid first step. At the end of the day, you don't have to justify your money decisions to anyone (other than those financially dependent on you). Everyone else doesn't get a say.

#4 Keep clear in your head the vision you have for a life well-lived. What does that look like for you? Where do you live, what do you do for fun, whom do you choose to spend your time with, and what do you do that lights you up? Too many of us, including me, have been guilty of chasing other people's vision of life, which doesn't fit. It's like trying to squeeze into a shoe that's a size smaller than your foot. It's going to hurt. Stop doing it. Live your life and live it well.

#5 Lastly, talking about money will revolutionize your relationship with money. It's why I named my podcast *Everyone's Talkin' Money*. Find a trusted group of friends with whom you can openly share your money thoughts, feelings, struggles, mistakes, and victories.

Can you imagine a world where it was okay to talk about money? I believe that's how we all collectively destigmatize money. Let's take money out of the shadows and stop letting money be the elephant in the room. Cultivate a healthy dialogue with your family and your partner around money. The best place to start is by asking, "Hey, how do you feel about money?"

I asked the oldest client I worked with, who was in his 90s, to share any words of wisdom with me about money and life that he wished he had heard himself. Here's what he said: "I made a lot of money. I wasted a lot of money. You can always make more money. What you can't get back is time. Time with your family, time with your friends, and time with yourself to enjoy being alive. If I could do it all over again, I'd focus more on how I spent my time than worrying about money, which dominated my life for far too many years. When I pass away, I hope people remember who I was and not how I spent my money."

That feels like a good place to leave the story.

One last thing, just in case you were wondering, here are my "Relationship with Money Is" answers. I thought it only seemed right to leave this chapter with one last bit of transparency.

. . .

YOUR RELATIONSHIP WITH MONEY IS. . .

A conversation with Shannah Game, Certified Financial Planner, Certified Trauma of Money Specialist, host of *Everyone's Talkin' Money* podcast

If you had to describe your relationship with money as a cartoon character, who would it be?

"I would say Linus from Peanuts. Linus is thoughtful and insightful and always there for his friends. He's also a really deep thinker, which I am in any area of life, but especially money. He does, of course, carry around a blanket for security. That's how I feel about my relationship with money. I want security, but have decided instead to focus on being hopeful at all times. I'm always reminding myself that money is just a tool and my feelings around that tool are always a choice."

What is one money mistake you haven't shared often?
"I've been an open book for most of my career and have shared so many mistakes. I passed up a bunch of career opportunities after college and running my film festival. I think back on them now and they all would've been a great fit for my skills and would've increased my bank account exponentially. I didn't take them because I was partly scared and partly entitled. If I could go back and do it over again, I'd jump at the chance to try out an opportunity before I turned it down."

What's one money splurge you're never giving up?
"Here's the thing about me, I don't splurge often. If I do splurge, I normally feel bad about it afterwards. But, I would say these days it's self-care that keeps me sane like massages, acupuncture, my sauna blanket, and I can't ever give up french fries."

. . .

QUESTIONS TO PONDER

1. What has been your biggest *aha* moment while reading this book?
2. What is the most significant change you've seen in your relationship with money?
3. Write out a commitment statement agreeing to keep your relationship with money unraveled. For example, "I promise to focus on healthy thoughts and feelings around money. I will create daily, weekly, and monthly action steps that help form good patterns and behaviors. I will dream big and not let money get in the way."

Resources

Many years ago, when I worked with my very first client, they asked, "Hey, do you have any exercises, tips, or suggestions you can offer to help me with my money after we work together?" I remember thinking, Oh, yeah, it's not enough that I solve your money issue; you need tools in your toolkit that you can come back to over and over again. That is how many of the Try This exercises were created in the book. Each client resonated with a different exercise so I just kept creating them. This money toolkit came from my deep desire to help everyone visualize and interact with their money from a healthier perspective going forward. I suggest giving the exercises and questions in the book a try. You'll figure out which ones are helpful and you can come back to those over and over again.

Here are some extra exercises and techniques you can try on your quest for a better relationship with money. My wish is that you try a few, learn from them, and then spread them to your friends and family so everyone can start to feel good about their money.

Box Breathing – Please do not underestimate the power of your breath when it comes to lowering money stress. I'm a breath holder and must remind myself to take deep breaths, frequently. The box breathing exercise is so helpful to regulate your central nervous system and to get your brain off of your money worries.

It works like this – breathe in for four counts, hold your breath for four counts, breathe out for four counts, and hold for four counts. It's breathing in a box-like pattern. You can repeat this pattern a few times and then check in with your body and nerves. See how different you feel just from breathing.

Box Breathing Benefits:

- Regulates autonomic nervous system
- Lowers blood pressure
- Gives a relaxed feeling in the mind and body

- Improves your mood
- Reduces stress
- Treats insomnia

Body Scan – This exercise involves paying attention to all the different areas of your body one by one. It's a great way to figure out where you store money stress in your body so you can work to relieve it. The Body Scan helps you get reintroduced to your body and its physical sensations. I turn to this exercise whenever I'm feeling overwhelmed by money (and life in general). As you notice feelings in your body, practice letting them go and accepting them as they are.

Sit or lie down in a comfortable position. You can close your eyes or keep them open. Feel into your body lying or sitting there. Feel into the areas where your body is making contact with the floor or whatever supports you. Feel your feet touching the ground. Feel where your legs, back, arms, and head touch the chair. Notice your breathing, entering and leaving your body. The purpose of the Body Scan is to be present with your body without wanting anything at all. You simply want to feel what is there. And, remember to breathe and just be present.

Starting at your feet, feel into each of them. Maybe feel your toes – are they tingling or warm or cold? Now, move your attention to your ankles and lower legs. What do you feel here? Perhaps you feel the fabric on your skin or your calves on your chair. Do you notice any tension? Can you release anything? Now, move up your knees and thighs. What do you feel here? Any pressure, temperature, or sensations that come to mind? Now, move up your pelvis and your belly. Is there any clinching in your waist? Moving up your spine, notice what you feel. Any tension areas or uncomfortable feelings? From there, move up to your hands and fingers. What do you feel? Any gripping or sensations? Now, move up your arms and neck. See what's going on there. Move to your face and your jaw. What does your face feel like? Are you clenching your jaw? Can you relax your eye muscles? Notice everything you're feeling. Take a breath in and out, and start to wiggle all your fingers and toes to bring them back to life. Stretch your body and notice what you feel after the exercise. You can do this exercise as often as you'd like to relax and release any tension.

Yoga Poses – Another way to mindfully combat stress in your daily life is to strike a pose – a yoga pose, of course. Constant stress in your life without a release valve will eventually take a toll on your body and mental health. Doing a simple yoga pose for just a few minutes a day to relieve stress has been shown to have a calming effect on the body. Stress zaps all of the energy in our bodies. When our energy tank is depleted, anxiety can build, and anything can push us over the edge (hello unexpected bill in the mail). Whether you are a regular practice veteran yogi or a newbie to yoga, doing these simple poses to relieve all that built-up stress will reap abundant rewards.

Child's pose

1. Kneel on a yoga mat or floor with legs together, sitting on your heels.
2. Hinge forward until your chest rests on your thighs, your forehead is on the floor
3. Curl your shoulders and let your hands rest, palms up, next to your feet, and hold for five breaths

Legs-Up-the-Wall pose

1. Sit with your hips against the wall and sit back, taking your legs up the wall
2. Your bottom should be pressed as close to the wall as possible
3. Hold for five minutes to release the pressure in your legs and feet (this is a great time to listen to some music or a meditation)

Corpse pose

1. Lie flat on your back with your legs together but not touching and your arms at your side, palms up
2. Keep your eyes closed and your face relaxed
3. Breathe deeply
4. Hold for three to five minutes

Daily Money Check-In – If you love to journal, this exercise is for you. It consists of six questions to ask yourself each morning and evening to bring focus and attention to your day. Even if you're not a journaler and have a wandering mind like myself, these six questions can help you center your thoughts. Exercises like this are great to do before you reach for your phone in bed.

Question 1 – How am I feeling this morning?

Question 2 – What is my daily goal? (You can list out multiple goals, but keep it to three or less)

Question 3 – What is my action step (or steps)?

Question 4 – What am I grateful for today?

Question 5 – What was today's moment of awesome (do this in the evening, and list out what went really well).

Question 6 – Word of the day (what word encapsulates this day)

1-2-3-4 Money Thought Exercise – I use this exercise frequently. Most of my thoughts about money are negative and not very affirming. But I felt so much better afterward whenever I turned to this exercise. Give it a try when you notice a negative thought bubble to the surface of your mind about money, your career, or your life in general.

Here's how it works:

Step 1 – When you have a negative thought, stop and ask yourself, is this thought true?

Step 2 – Then ponder – Can you tell if this thought is really 100% true (or is there some degree of falsity)?

Step 3 – How do you feel when you believe this thought?

Step 4 – Who would you be without this thought? (This is a powerful part of separating yourself from negative thoughts.)

The point of this exercise is to challenge your automatic thoughts and help you sort through which thoughts are helpful and which are harmful to you. The more you practice this process, the better you'll be at recognizing negative self-talk in the moment.

Wouldn't It Be Cool If List – I was introduced to this exercise by a mentor, and I've shared it countless times. Too often, we limit what we do in life because of money. You think, "If I only had more money, I could do that." The Wouldn't It Be Cool If List asks you to think beyond money and imagine everything you want to do in life. It's a place to dream and envision.

It's a simple exercise. Get out a sheet of paper and set a timer for 15 minutes. Write down as many things as you'd like to do (that would be cool to do) without thinking about money as an objection. Go crazy on this list. When the timer is up, look back at your list and ask yourself, what's in my way of doing the things on this list? If your answer is money, I want you to stop right there. For example, while you might not be able to buy a secluded island and never work again, you can look at your current career and income and see if there is a way to better that situation. You might be surprised at how motivated you feel once you create your Wouldn't It Be Cool If List to start taking action steps in your life. I have my list hung on my wall, and it reminds me to think beyond money and that life is meant to be enjoyed.

PODCASTS AND BOOKS

I've also been able to interview thousands of people on my podcast over the last 10 years. All of them amazing and worth a listen. If there's anything you want to learn about money, I've got an episode for you. Many of these experts have amazing books and podcasts that you need to listen to. Here are some of my favorites in each category.

PODCASTS

My list of podcast recommendations could span miles. Podcasts are such a great way to learn about money topics in an engaging and approachable way. Pick a topic that you want to learn about and I guarantee you there are loads of episodes to help you. These are some of the podcasts that make my regular rotation.

- *Everyone's Talkin' Money* (shameless self-plug)
- *The Stacking Benjamins Show*
- *Mind Money Balance*
- *Earn and Invest*
- *Money Nerds*
- *50 Fires*
- *AffordAnything*
- *Money Isn't Scary*
- *BiggerPockets Money*
- *BiggerPockets Real Estate*
- *Catching up to FI*
- *The Personal Finance Podcast*
- *Unf*ck Your Brain*
- *Terrible, Thanks for Asking*
- *So Money*
- *True Home Confessions*
- *Seed Money*
- *WorkParty*

BOOKS TO READ

If you want more financial education, there are many amazing books to choose from. These are a few of my favorites, written by some of my favorite money experts. You can't go wrong by reading any of these books.

- *Happy Money* by Ken Honda
- *Happy Money, Happy Life* by Jason Vitug
- *The Soul of Money* by Lynne Twist
- *Plant Your Money Tree* by Michele Schneider
- *Ask Questions, Save Money, Make More* by Matt Schulz
- *Get Good with Money* by Tiffany Aliche

- *Don't Leave Money on the Table* by Jacqueline Twillie
- *Invest Like a Girl* by Jessica Spangler
- *The Psychology of Money* by Morgan Housel
- *The Simple Path to Wealth* by J L Collins
- *The One-Page Financial Plan* by Carl Richards
- *Tipped* by Barbara Sloan
- *The Art of Money* by Bari Tessler
- *Your Journey to Financial Freedom* by Jamila Souffrant
- *Finance for the People* by Paco De Leon
- *Keeping Finance Personal* by Ellyce Fulmore
- *Broke Millennial* by Erin Lowry

QUESTIONS TO ASK YOURSELF

I've included a bunch of questions to ask yourself after each chapter. Here are 25 additional questions to ponder. As I mentioned, I keep a separate journal for my money thoughts and questions. It's a great resource to look back on and see your progress.

1. My money fears are. . .
2. What are you grateful for?
3. Write yourself a money pep talk.
4. How do you define wealth?
5. Who is your money mentor, and why?
6. How much money is enough?
7. What is your vision for your life?
8. If you received $1,000,000 today, how would you spend it?
9. What if everything with your money went okay? How would that make you feel?
10. How did your family approach saving, spending, and giving away money as a kid?
11. What has your experience been with credit card debt?

12. How is money currently impacting your life?

13. What makes you feel fulfilled in life? (Are you doing enough of that?)

14. What's the best thing you've spent money on?

15. What's one money mistake you wish you could get a do-over for?

16. What money messages do you remember from your childhood?

17. What was your first job experience like?

18. What were your money thoughts today?

19. What would you be doing for a living if money weren't a thing?

20. What's your biggest money splurge that you're never giving up?

21. What are your money goals for the next year?

22. How do you *want* to feel about money and what's in the way?

23. What's one thing you really want to learn about money?

24. How would you describe your relationship to money as a cartoon character? (This is my favorite question to ask guests on my podcast.)

25. What do you want your future money story to be?

All of the exercises in this book are here to support you. I hope they have brought some relief to you along your journey. Keep coming back to them. Remember, your relationship with money is a journey, not a destination. I'll be here cheering you on.

Acknowledgments

I am eternally grateful to those who helped me bring this book to life. First, I want to sincerely thank all my loyal *Everyone's Talkin' Money* podcast listeners over the years. You all have enriched my life in ways you will never know. Thanks for helping make this little podcast that could earn its spot in the top 0.5% of all podcasts worldwide. You have listened all around the world, shared episodes, written questions, and, most importantly, learned about money from some of the finest people around whom I've been fortunate enough to interview. Thank you for believing in me and helping me in turn to believe in myself. Ten years ago, when I plugged in my microphone, I never imagined that you'd still be listening and learning. My only goal is to be able to enrich your life and show you that we all struggle with this thing called money.

I also want to thank all my clients and students who have trusted me with their money, education, and advice. I take great pride in this privilege of being able to spread financial literacy and help you all stress a little less about money.

I want to give a big, heartfelt thanks to my agent, Karen Murgolo, at Aevitas Creative Management, for championing this book and my voice. I spent a lot of time looking for an agent who would understand my perspective on money, and I'm so lucky to have found you. You saw something in me and allowed me to explore and develop this idea from start to finish.

I look forward to many more books together, hint, hint.

Kevin Harreld, thank you for breathing life into this book and everyone on the Wiley team who spent hours shaping and refining the words I put on paper. I'm so glad I found a fellow Hoosier to work with.

Everyone needs a friend like Valerie Zell. She has been my ride-or-die since college and helped me bring another one of my ideas to life: Hometown Cinema, my film festival. Valerie, you are a whiz with words, and you encouraged me to dig deeper into each page of this book. Sometimes, you know my voice better than I do. Without your guidance, support, and input, this book wouldn't be what it is.

Sometimes, you are lucky enough to find someone who turns from mentor to friend to family. Diana Wilson, you are the cherry on top, and I couldn't be more thankful for your presence in my life. I'm not sure how we met, but I'm thanking my lucky stars for it happening. You've taught me that ideas are just ideas until you dare to step forward and take action. I've learned so much from your dedication to excellence and sheer fortitude as you tackle every endeavor in life. Most of all, thank you for sharing your humanness with me and seeing me for who I am beyond any accolades or the size of my bank account. May this next chapter of life be the best for us both.

My circle of friends is small but deep, and I wouldn't be where I am without you all. Amanda Dinan, thanks for chasing me down the street and asking if our dogs could meet. You have a forever membership in my tribe, my friend. You were one of the first to read a few scribbled words on paper as I started this book-writing journey and encouraged me all the way. I promise to bring you along the day I get to meet Hoda Kotb and all the fine folks at the *TODAY* show.

Amy Wrenn, I'll meet you for French Fry Fridays any day of the week. Thanks for seeing me and for becoming the unofficial yet still official sister I always wanted. Let's go take over the world, okay?

Also, for my dear friend Shannon French, who passed away more than eight years ago from stage-four double metastatic breast cancer. You were so passionate about financial literacy and gave so much to this world. I know you were present with each word I put on these pages. I hope I've done you justice and you're smiling up above. I will miss you forever.

There aren't enough words to properly thank my parents, Stan and Cindy Compton. Besides being the whole reason I'm alive, you are the best parents anyone could ask for. You have always encouraged me to explore my talents and patiently sat through all my "concerts" as I developed my creativity when I was younger. I surely wouldn't have the career I do without my dad, and my mom is just about the best cheerleader you could ever ask for. Thanks for all your morale, financial, and loving support over the years.

I want to thank two of the most special people in my life. My husband, Jeff Game, you are a creative powerhouse and have brought me so much joy. Thank you for making me laugh when I don't want to and gently encouraging me to enjoy life and be present. (Even though I'm still a work in progress.) How about we do some more cool stuff together?

Winnie Stardust Game, I know you are just a 44lb mini Mountain Goldendoodle dog, but girl, you have taught me so much about life, happiness, balance, and owning your uniqueness. Thanks for all those licks and furry hugs on days when I struggled to find the words.

I want to send a special shout-out to all the misfits, square pegs trying to fit in round holes, and road-less-traveled readers. I've never felt like I fit into the traditional mold of what a financial expert looks like. I've longed to be "normal," but then I realized that normal is whatever I make of it. I want you never to lose your spirit. I want you to always push against the status quo. I want you to dare to dream big and not let anyone tell you otherwise. And I want you to stay true to what wealth looks like for you, whether living in a shiny apartment in a big city, a cozy abode in a small town, or something in between. Chase after your dreams. Write that book. Launch that business. Share your beauty with the world.

Lastly, a big shout-out to my bright and shiny writing cape that I wore while writing this book. You've been there through all the long hours of writing and reminded me that I can do it, word by word.

About the Author

Shannah Game is a Transformational Money Expert, Host of *Everyone's Talkin' Money*, named a Top 4 Money Podcast by *The New York Times* with more than 26 million downloads worldwide, Certified Financial Planner™, Certified Trauma of Money Specialist, and multi-passionate entrepreneur with an MBA. She started her first business in college at Indiana University, one of the first student film festivals, named Hometown Cinema, which helped more than 500 students get jobs and internships in the entertainment industry. She's also been named an Outstanding Young Californian and received a 40 Under 40 award. Shannah's mission is to talk openly about the other side of money: the power of your thoughts and feelings and how those keep you hostage from reaching your money goals. *Unraveling Your Relationship with Money* is her love letter to you, helping you radically change your relationship with money so you can let go of money shame and fear and finally feel good about money (or at least a bit better). Shannah is a sought-after financial writer and speaker, and her financial expertise has been highlighted in articles for *The New York Times*, *The Cut*, *Women's Health*, *MSN Money*, *Reuters*, *Refinery 29*, *Yahoo! Finance*, *theSkimm*, and *Real Simple*, to name a few. She spent 10 years as a Lecturer in Finance at California State University Northridge, where she taught more than 3,500 students and was awarded a Golden Apple Teaching Award for her dedication to financial literacy. Shannah suffers from single-sided deafness and has become a mental health advocate for those with invisible disabilities. She lives in Asheville, North Carolina, with her husband, Jeff, and their beloved dog, Winnie Stardust.

Index